KNOWING CHRISTIANITY

RELIGION AND SCIENCE

KNOWING CHRISTIANITY

A series edited by Dr. William Neil to provide for thinking laymen a solid but non-technical presentation of what the Christian religion is and what it has to say.

The first titles are:

THE CHRISTIAN FAITH
THE OLD TESTAMENT
THE LIFE AND TEACHING OF JESUS
GOD IN THE NEW TESTAMENT
THE EARLY CHURCH
FAITH AND PHILOSOPHY
CHRISTIANITY AND OTHER RELIGIONS
THE CHRISTIAN FATHERS
THE ATONEMENT
CHRISTIAN ETHICS
THE ROOTS OF THE RADICAL THEOLOGY
CHRISTIAN APOLOGETICS
CHRISTIANITY: A PSYCHOLOGIST'S TRANSLATION
THE NEW TESTAMENT

KNOWING CHRISTIANITY

RELIGION AND SCIENCE

by
JOHN HABGOOD
M.A., Ph.D.
Principal of The Queen's College
Birmingham

HODDER AND STOUGHTON
LONDON   SYDNEY   AUCKLAND   TORONTO

EDITOR'S PREFACE

To judge by the unending flow of religious literature from the various publishing houses there is an increasingly large demand on the part of ordinary intelligent people to know more about what Christianity has to say. This series is designed to help meet this need and to cater for just this kind of people.

It assumes there is a growing body of readers, inside and outside the Church, prepared to give serious attention to the nature and claims of the Christian faith, and who expect to be given by theologians authoritative and up-to-date answers to the kind of questions thinking people want to ask.

More and more it becomes clear that we are unlikely to get any answers that will satisfy the deepest needs of the human spirit from any other quarter. Present-day science and philosophy give us little help on the ultimate questions of human destiny. Social, political and educational panaceas leave most of us unpersuaded. If we are not to end our quest for the truth about ourselves and the world we live in in cynicism and disillusionment where else can we turn but to religion.

Too often in the past two thousand years the worst advertisement for Christianity has been its supporters and advocates. Yet alone of all the great world religions it has shown that a faith which was oriental in origin could be transplanted into the Western world and from there strike root again in the East. The present identification of Christianity in the minds of Asians and Africans with European culture and Western capitalism or imperialism is a passing phase. To say that no other religion has the same potentialities as a world-wide faith for everyman is neither to denigrate the God-given truth in Buddhism, Islam and the rest, nor to say that at this stage Christianity as generally practised and understood in the West presents much more than a caricature of its purpose.

Perhaps the best corrective to hasty judgement is to measure these two thousand years against the untold millions of years of man's development. Organised Christianity is still in its infancy, as is the mind of man as he seeks to grapple with truths that could only come to him by revelation. The half has not yet been told and the full implications for human thought and action of the coming of God in Christ have as yet been only dimly grasped by most of us.

It is as a contribution to a deeper understanding of the mystery that surrounds us that this series is offered. The early volumes deal, as is only right, with fundamental issues—the historical impact of Christianity upon mankind based upon its Jewish origins and establishing itself in the wider world; the essence of the Christian faith and the character of Christian behaviour. Later volumes in the series will deal with various aspects of Christian thought and practice in relation to human life in all its variety and with its perennial problems.

The intention is to build up a library which under the general title of "Knowing Christianity" will provide for thinking laymen a solid but non-technical presentation of what the Christian religion is and what it has to say in this atomic age.

The writers invited to contribute to this series are not only experts in their own fields but are all men who are deeply concerned that the gulf should be bridged between the specialised studies of the theologian and the untheologically minded average reader who nevertheless wants to know what theology has to say. I am sure that I speak in the name of all my colleagues in this venture when I express the hope that this series will do much to bridge the gap.

The University, Nottingham   WILLIAM NEIL

CONTENTS

	Page
Editor's Preface	v

Chapter

1.	The Untidiness of Life	9
2.	The Foundations of Science	14
3.	The Break-up of the Old Order	22
4.	The New Synthesis	32
5.	Problems of Space	40
6.	Theological Reaction	48
7.	Life	56
8.	Nothing but Apes?	64
9.	Science and the Bible	72
10.	The Limits of Doubt	80
11.	The Rise of Technology	88
12.	Minds and Machines	94
13.	After Freud	102
14.	The Boundaries of Nature	110
15.	Maps	118
16.	The Scientific Attitude	127
17.	Types of Knowledge	136
18.	Religious Dogma	144
	Bibliography	152

Chapter 1

THE UNTIDINESS OF LIFE

Some people claim that there is a fundamental conflict between science and the Christian faith. They claim that as science has advanced, so Christianity has retreated. They believe we have now come to the point at which dogmatic religion can be seen to have no future; it may still be fighting a rearguard action, but to all intents and purposes it is obsolete, clung to only by those who are so stupid that they cannot see the arguments against it, or so clever that they can make up spurious reasons of their own for continuing to believe.

Other people believe that although there have been times of conflict between the two, these have been caused more by misunderstandings than by deep and irreconcilable divisions. Such people often point to the nineteenth century as an example of a time when much bitterness and controversy on these matters could have been avoided. All would have been well, they think, if the followers of Darwin had been less sweeping in their claims for the theory of evolution, and theologians had been less literal-minded in their interpretation of the Bible.

A third class of people regards such controversies as essentially trivial, storms in Victorian teacups. These people are more impressed by the sense in which science itself can be seen as a religious activity. Science, they say, reveals the wisdom of God in the order of creation. On this view, the theory of evolution, so far from being a difficulty, is an inspiration, a revelation of the scale and grandeur of the purposes of God. Science is a quest for truth, and all truth is ultimately God's truth.

All three points of view stress something important. But the position I want to put forward in this book is yet a fourth one, which at first sight seems a good deal less attractive than any of the others. It takes a little from all of them. From the first view it takes the belief that there is a sense in which science and religion must always be in conflict; but it does not go on to draw the conclusion that religion is therefore obsolete. In the light of the second view, it recognises that people can sometimes fight for good reasons about the wrong thing; but this is not a com-

9

plete explanation of all the conflicts. If we were able to see the whole truth through the eyes of God, doubtless such conflicts as remain would finally disappear; this is what the third viewpoint is showing us. But since we cannot see through the eyes of God, and are not likely to be able to do so, it seems a little premature to treat all the conflicts as if they had been resolved. We must therefore live with them.

It is the assertion that we must learn to live with a certain amount of conflict and untidiness, which is the essence of the fourth view. I believe that there are no final answers to many of the traditional problems of science and religion, and that we oversimplify our actual experience of life if we ignore one or the other of them, or imagine that the conflict between them is of the kind in which one side or the other must win.

Perhaps this may seem highly unsatisfactory. Most people who think about such matters at all want a way of looking at the world which makes sense of it as a whole. Untidiness is distrusted, and sometimes with good reason; it can be a cover for intellectual sloppiness. One of the main defences against error has always been the search for consistency. Men have tried to build systems of thought which hang together and in which there is a place for everything. Such systems have the additional advantage of providing a firm basis for action; and this may be the secret of their popularity among those who are not intellectually-minded. People look to parties or creeds or slogans which claim to provide definite answers to the questions which perplex them. Is Christianity true or false? It would make life so much simpler if one could answer yes or no.

Unfortunately, however, experience very rarely gives us answers of that kind. Science achieves its successes by restricting its questions to those to which straight answers can be given. This is one of the main reasons for its attractiveness. It provides definite information in a limited field. The only trouble is that its questions are not always the most interesting and relevant ones for our lives; and when scientists try to ask those particular questions they become just as confused as anybody else. There seems to be a frustrating law that the more vital the questions we ask, the vaguer and more varied are the answers we can expect.

Life, in other words, is a compromise, a balancing of claims and insights. At first most of us are justifiably unwilling to accept this sort of compromise; we tend to be impetuous and dogmatic; we want to find truth definitely here and not there; and when we cannot find it, there is a temptation to react in an exaggerated way by saying that there is no truth to be found anywhere. Much modern literature reflects this attitude, with its rather strident cynicism and over-emphasis on human bewilderment.

In traditional thought, wisdom lies on the far side of such impetuousness. The wise are those who have learnt to find truth in many different places; who have enough stability not to be thrown off their balance by the latest fads and discoveries; who know the limits of their knowledge, but have a humble certainty about the truths by which they live.

Few people attain to the heights of wisdom, and it is all too easy to put on a show of wisdom which is, in fact, no more than a flabby and muddled conservatism. But it is possible, I believe, without making any great claims for oneself, to pursue knowledge in such a way that something of its many-sidedness emerges willy-nilly; and this is an important first step to wisdom, even though the goal may be very distant indeed. All that is needed is a readiness to sympathise with different points of view, and a willingness to dig before one starts to build. If these qualities are to the fore, then those who are prepared to tolerate a certain amount of intellectual untidiness can be protected against the charge of dishonesty or incompetence.

This book is an attempt to discuss science and religion in the belief that today is a day for digging rather than for building. It is not a systematic defence of the Christian faith, although there are themes and arguments which run through the length of it. Each chapter is intended to provide a discussion of some scientific or religious issue, and only in the last few chapters is there any attempt at constructive and consistent argument. The impression which I hope will be formed is that the debate between the religious and scientific ways of approaching experience is an important and a continuing one; and that, while there are no final answers to some of the questions concerning their relationship, this need not prevent a person from being both an honest Christian and an honest scientist.

I shall approach the subject historically, because we can only understand the present relationship between science and religion, and some of our spontaneous feelings about that relationship, in the light of the past. If we were simply concerned to study two rival systems of thought, their historical development might not matter to us greatly. But one of the facts which will become apparent is that neither science nor religion can be studied in the abstract; they are both ways of thinking and acting adopted by particular men in particular circumstances. It is true that scientific discoveries are what they are, and should not be affected by the personality of the discoverer; but the ways in which they have been used, and the effects they have had on men's feelings about the universe, are very much matters of history. And this is the level at which they impinge on religion. My approach, therefore, is historical, and the chapters are arranged in rough chronological order.

History by itself is not enough, though. Nothing is more frustrating than a book which sets out to discuss our modern perplexities, and which illuminates their historical background, but does absolutely nothing to point the way through them. That there are modern perplexities I take for granted. Some years ago there was a cartoon in the *New Yorker* which showed a mother and her son at the toy counter in a large department store; the assistant was saying, "Now, madam, this toy is ideally suited to teach your child to live in the modern world. Whichever way you try to put it together, it doesn't fit." The assistant's remark was an almost perfect commentary on the novels of Kafka, and Kafka himself could be called the father of much that is most characteristic in modern literature. His novels describe a baffling world which always seems to be on the verge of making sense, but never does. They bite deeply into the minds of those who read them, because they force the uncomfortable reflection that Kafka's world might be their own. If we can take the pulse of an age by looking at its novels it seems obvious that the dominant themes today are of meaninglessness and despair. They describe a world whose parts do not fit together.

Though it would not be true to say that one of the causes of this is the growth of science, yet science is somehow bound up with it. It is science which has helped us so to sharpen our critical faculties that we can embark on an unlimited programme of debunking. It is science which has had a major share in the transformation of man's understanding of the universe, a transformation which has left man himself unsure of his own position or the meaning of his life. I have no desire to cast science as the villain of the piece, because the benefits it has brought have been overwhelming. Nevertheless, as a purely objective statement of fact, it seems to me that the growth of science has brought its problems as well as its advantages, and we have not yet learnt to adjust ourselves to the changes. A book on science and religion ought to concern itself, therefore, with some of these problems as they affect us today.

One final point. Any book on religion, especially by a clergyman, is bound to appear biased. I have already said that I propose to set out a certain view of the relation between science and religion, and I have already used the words "religion" and "Christian faith" as if they were interchangeable. Critical readers may have felt that the language had an ominous ring of special pleading, that my conclusions have been dictated in advance, and that I am assuming without argument that the only religion worth considering is Christianity.

I draw attention to this because I believe it is impossible to discuss religion without some element of pleading either for or against it. Our religion is what we are committed to, what we feel most strongly about; its object is the object of our worship. To try to discuss it purely objectively as a system of thought, or as something believed and practised by somebody else, is not really to get to grips with it at all. Of course, there is a great deal to be learnt about it simply as a phenomenon, and any Christian who wishes to defend his faith would do well to be as objective about it as possible; but in the end the only people who can fully appreciate a religion are those who live by it. I believe it is safer, therefore, to be honest about one's convictions at the start, rather than to pretend to enjoy an impartiality and omniscience which are in fact unattainable. It then becomes possible to write about what one knows from within, and to allow one's readers to correct for bias if they feel it necessary.

I have tried to use the word "religion" when discussing "the religious phenomenon", the word "theology" when discussing its intellectual content, and the phrase "Christian faith" when writing explicitly about Christianity or from a more personal point of view. But these elements cannot be completely disentangled, nor is my usage entirely consistent. Not even religion by itself, let alone religion in its relation to science, can be divided up into tidy compartments.

Chapter 2

THE FOUNDATIONS OF SCIENCE

Science, like a great many other things in Western civilisation, began with the Greeks. But it is an odd fact that one of the great enemies of modern science in its early years was the residual influence of Greek thought. How this came to be so is the theme of this chapter.

The Greeks possessed one priceless insight which was the clue to much of their achievement. They believed in reason. They believed that the world made sense, and that rational thought could discover its secrets. Obviously this belief is of fundamental importance if any science is to be possible at all. Without some sort of underlying trust that the world is not completely haphazard, nobody could begin to be a scientist; where there is no conception of law and order in nature there can be no science. This is why science could never have arisen in a society which took polytheism seriously. Where anything can happen because a whimsical god decides to do it, the wise man concentrates on keeping on the right side of the gods; there is no point in his trying to find the laws of nature because, according to his beliefs, they do not exist.

Although the Greeks were superficially polytheists, their belief in the orderliness of things went much deeper than their polytheism. They believed, too, in the power of pure thought. Hence they were fascinated by mathematics, and it is in this sphere that some of their greatest discoveries lie. Mathematics is not only a supreme example of orderliness; it is also, like philosophy, one of the few branches of learning in which it is possible to produce impressive results simply by sitting and thinking. For a race which was always a little suspicious of manual labour, this undoubtedly gave mathematics an additional lustre. But their concern about it was amply justified. Greek geometry, which is still the basis of modern geometry, is a prodigious example of what pure thought can achieve.

In this environment science could flourish—up to a point. Geometrical analysis was applied to problems in physics, astronomy and engineering, and thus began the link between science and mathematics which has been one of the most fruitful of all the developments of the scientific method. Nowadays science without mathematics is inconceivable. Some scientists feel this so strongly that they hardly deign to call a subject "scientific" unless its results can be expressed mathematically. According to such scientists psycho-analytic theory, for example, is still "pre-scientific".

Why this should be so is not difficult to see. The aim of every scientist is to understand the phenomena he is studying. But this at once raises the question, what do we mean by "understanding" something? The stock answer is to say that we understand the unknown by explaining it in terms of the known. Thus we understand a bit about the planets when we think of them as being like stones whirled round on the ends of strings held by the sun. Such an explanation we call "a scientific model". Everybody knows that this particular model is extremely crude and unsatisfactory, even though it once had its usefulness. Science advances as scientists search for more and more satisfactory models, and obviously the more a model itself is understood, the more satisfactory it is.

The only completely satisfactory model would be one which could itself be completely understood. And that is why mathematics is so important. The whole point of mathematics is that it is a system of thought which can be completely understood. This does not, of course, imply that every luckless individual trying to make sense of it is guaranteed to succeed; all that is claimed is that anybody who is sufficiently intelligent and who follows the rules of mathematics, is bound to arrive at the same results as everybody else. Thus, while it is possible to argue the pros and cons of a model of the solar system in terms of strings and stones, as soon as the movements of the planets are translated into precise mathematical terms no more argument is necessary. So long as we accept Newton's inverse square law, then we can calculate the movements of the planets which it predicts; and these predictions follow logically and exactly from the law. Insofar as we understand one, we understand the other. In deducing the movements from the law, the explanation which mathematics gives us is complete.

Mathematics is thus an immensely powerful tool in the hands of scientists. The whole laborious business of trying to work out what to expect if a certain hypothesis were true, begins to become manageable when it can be translated into mathematical terms. Think, for example, how impossible it would be to predict an eclipse of the sun without using mathematics; the procedure would be incredibly complex. In fact, modern science has only grown to the extent it has through the parallel advance of mathematics. The calculus was developed by Newton to help his calculations of the orbits of the planets; statistics arrived in time to provide a basis for thermodynamics; and non-Euclidean geometry was invented as a piece of pure speculation just before Einstein wanted it for the theory of relativity. But this is to anticipate. The only points to note at the moment are that science and mathematics are very closely interrelated, and that the Greeks were good mathematicians.

Unfortunately, however, there is one dangerous feature in the partnership between science and mathematics. Mathematics can all too easily become the senior partner. This happened as early as the time of Pythagoras in the sixth century B.C. The Pythagoreans were so impressed by the power of mathematics that they thought they could disclose the secrets of the world simply by studying the properties of numbers and geometrical figures. The sphere is the perfect shape; therefore the heavenly bodies must be spherical. Ten is a highly significant number; therefore there must be ten heavenly bodies, no more, no less. And this is a great mistake. It is a failure to realise that mathematics is essentially abstract. It is about the relations between things, and not about things in particular. A mathematical problem about six oranges is not basically different from a similar problem about six elephants or six giant marrows; what matters is the number six. When we begin a textbook problem about a hippopotamus sliding down a frictionless grass slope, the first thing we do is to forget the hippopotamus and the grass, and concentrate on the angle of the slope. This may seem very dull and unimaginative; but the fact is that mathematics is about numbers and functions and lines and angles and logical operations; maybe this is why it sometimes seems rarefied and remote to ordinary people who would much rather be thinking about hippopotami.

Be that as it may, the crucial question is this. Can a branch of learning so essentially abstract as mathematics tell us anything about the real world? The answer depends on our philosophy, on what we mean by "real". Many of the Greeks, especially those who followed Plato, answered, "Yes, it can." For them the real world was not our world of ordinary experience at all. It was the world of perfect "forms" or "ideas". They believed that our world is only an imperfect shadow of this perfect reality, which can be known by pure thought alone. The highest expression of pure thought, the most successful attempt to wrestle with pure forms, is to be found in mathematics. Therefore mathematics is the clue to reality; it is the ideal means of explanation.

From the point of view of modern science, this is both true, and disastrously false. True, because as we have already seen, there is a sense in which mathematics *is* the ideal means of explanation. Disastrously false, in that it directed men's attention away from the world of ordinary experience, what we now call the empirical world, and made them concentrate on what they thought it *ought to be like*, rather than on what experience showed it to be like. Because the circle is the perfect form, they argued, therefore the planets must revolve round the sun in circles. Men believed this for centuries, and it took the most enormous effort to break the belief. Kepler, the man who finally deduced the elliptical orbits of the planets, almost killed himself with mathematical exertion before he could even bring himself to conceive that their orbits were not circles of some kind.

Mathematics, in other words, is double-faced in relation to science. On the one hand, it is an enormous help and stimulus. It holds out the prospect of making sense of things. On the other hand, it can become a dangerous mistress. It can tempt men into thinking that because an idea is simple, because it makes sense mathematically, therefore there is no need to bother about actual experience, or to undertake the laborious business of unravelling complicated facts. Nor was it only a temptation to the Greeks. There are still those who are tempted this way. Perhaps the most famous modern example is the great physicist, Eddington, who believed that he could deduce the basic physical constants from purely theoretical considerations about the way in which physicists measure things. Most scientists would deny that this is possible, even in principle. Mathematics is one thing; and the facts of nature are another. Where mathematics is allowed its head too much, objective science stops and speculation takes its place. This is one of the reasons why Greek science petered out.

There was, however, another tradition of Greek science which at first sight might look as though it could have redressed the balance. Aristotle was in many ways the direct opposite of Plato, even though he was his pupil. He was not nearly so enthusiastic about mathematics; nor did he concern himself with Plato's world of perfect forms and ideas. He was a scientist, as Plato was not, and his aim, like that of any modern scientist, was to make sense of the world of nature. Where he agreed with Plato was in his belief that the world was rational, that it was the creation of an orderly mind, and hence that it was worth investigating.

His range was immense. He created the science of logic. He wrote on philosophy, ethics, politics, physics, astronomy, medicine and natural history. Mathematics was the only subject he avoided. Because he believed that nature was an orderly whole, he set out to demonstrate its structure in as many branches of knowledge as he could. As a result he produced one of the most impressive systems of thought the world has ever known, so impressive, in fact, that it dominated the mind of the Western world for 2,000 years, and is still used by some philosophers today.

One of the keys to his thought is his analysis of causality. He divided causes into two main classes, final and efficient, and believed that the really interesting and important causes are the "final" ones.

We can make the distinction clear with a practical example. Supposing somebody were to ask why a space capsule is whirling round the earth, two kinds of answer would be possible. We could say, first, that it is in space because it was shot there by a rocket, that it has such and such a velocity because the rocket had such and such a thrust; and so on. This would be to give an "efficient cause" of its motions; it would explain it in terms of what had made it happen, or "effected" it. On the other hand we might say that the space capsule is where it is to boost Russian or American prestige, or to investigate the properties of outer space. This would be to give a "final" cause of its motion; it would be to explain it in terms of the purpose of space capsules and man's intentions in launching them; we should be thinking about the realm of "ends". Hence the word "final".

For Aristotle, to make sense of nature was to see it in terms of "ends" or "purposes". He thought of things as behaving in the way they do because this is their "nature", this is how they fit into the grand cosmic scheme. He was more interested in why things happen than in how they happen. He was satisfied to say that stones fall to the ground because they are heavy, and it is the "nature" of heavy objects to seek the lowest place. A mathematical analysis of the dynamics of falling bodies (i.e. a study of its efficient causes) would have seemed to him unnecessary and irrelevant, not really getting to the heart of the matter at all. Such an analysis would soon be bogged down in the purely incidental features of a highly complex situation. It seemed much more sensible to ask general questions about the nature of things. The only way to construct a really comprehensive system of thought is to concentrate on general principles and ignore the masses of detail.

In biology such an approach is reasonably helpful. The search for final causes can lead to a lot of interesting discoveries. There is some point in asking "why" as well as "how" when dealing with animals.

The question, "Why do the most intelligent animals walk on two legs rather than on four?" is not misleading or ridiculous. It can have a perfectly sensible answer; for instance, only two-legged creatures can manipulate objects with their hands, and so do not need enormous mouths and jaws to act as weapons, and so can avoid having big jaw muscles with correspondingly large bones covering the skull, and so have more room for a large brain which can balance in a fairly light, bony covering on an upright spine. In other words, one of the advantages of walking upright is that it allows the development of a large brain. Most biologists would undoubtedly want to say a great deal more about the upright posture, for example, about its evolutionary history, its mechanics and its anatomy. But as far as it goes the explanation in terms of purposes, the attempt to see where standing upright fits in with the general plan of animal structure, makes good sense. And in fact, biology is riddled with this kind of explanation.

However, what may be useful up to a point in biology, may be wildly inappropriate in physics. To say that a stone falls to the ground because it seeks the lowest place, does not really help anybody. And to talk, as Aristotle did in another context, about "nature abhorring a vacuum" may be a graphic way of describing some of the effects of atmospheric pressure, but it led research in the wrong direction for centuries.

Physics only began to make real progress when men became more interested in efficient than in final causes; when they asked, "How do stones fall?" and tried to answer in terms of velocity and distance, rather than by making general statements about "heaviness". Aristotle had been asking the wrong questions; questions which are plausible enough if one is concerned with a whole philosophy of nature, and may be helpful up to a point in biology, but in the end block scientific progress.

Nevertheless he was not wholly wrong. This is one of the curious features of Greek science, that it was such a medley of valuable and obstructive ideas. Everybody knows nowadays that science feeds on facts; most modern scientific theories rely on an immense number of detailed measurements of a kind the Greeks never made. But Aristotle had a shrewd sense that the mere accumulation of facts is not enough; it is all too easy to get lost in the details of an imperfect world. Newton would never have been able to propose his laws of motion if he had tried to take into account all the detailed differences made by friction, air resistance and gravity in any actual experiment with moving bodies. In fact in most great scientific discoveries there has been an element of oversimplification, a deliberate concentration on certain facts to the exclusion of others, even a willingness to consider ideal states, like frictionless, gravitation-free motion which cannot be reproduced in a laboratory. The trouble with Aristotle was not that he thought about ideal states. We with our frictionless hippopotami do exactly the same. The trouble was that he grossly underestimated the number of facts which are necessary before making generalisations about nature; he built his system on foundations that were too flimsy, and the final result of his genius was to fossilise science for 2,000 years.

In this chapter we have seen something of the extraordinary double-sidedness of the Greek contribution to science. It was so wonderfully right in its sense of the importance of mathematics, its belief in reason, its conviction that the world made sense. And on the other hand it was so heart-breakingly wrong in its reliance on reason alone, in its concern for the wrong kind of causality, in its underestimate of the complexity of the world of facts.

When in later chapters we consider Christian thought in its relation to science, we shall find the same double-sidedness, the same rightness and wrongness. To have traced out a few of the tangled threads of Greek science may serve as a warning against dismissing one side or the other too quickly when sincere and intelligent men are found to disagree. Few such men are wholly mistaken in what they believe.

Chapter 3

THE BREAK-UP OF THE OLD ORDER

The beginnings of modern science in the sixteenth and seventeenth centuries caused changes in men's thinking about the universe, as great as any that have ever taken place. As in most revolutions, the changes were marked by unsettlement, fear, controversy and persecution. If we are to understand these reactions, we must try to get some glimpse of what was at stake.

Mediaeval men lived between earth and heaven at the centre of God's universe. Above them were the stars and planets circling in their crystal spheres; this was the realm of perfection where there was neither change nor decay. The heavenly bodies moved in perfect circles, the only kind of motion proper to a changeless and incorruptible reality. Below men were the animals, made for man's use and instruction; and below the animals were the various lower orders of creation, right down to inanimate earth. The earth was made of a lower kind of stuff than heaven. It was corruptible; it could be changed; it had been spoilt by sin. Nevertheless, it had been made by God to be the place where man should dwell; hence it all made sense; there was a plan behind it. Some bits of the plan, like the meaning of the rainbow as the sign of God's faithfulness, had been revealed in Scripture; other bits were obscure. But the important thing was that men felt themselves to be at home in a relatively small universe which had been created largely for their benefit.

Such was the picture which science was to shatter. It was a picture which owed a great deal to Aristotle, whose ideas of plan and purpose had fitted very well with a Christian interpretation of creation. But by the end of the Middle Ages, centuries after he had written, Aristotle's hand lay like a dead weight on all attempts to think freshly about the structure of nature. It was only as men's respect for authority began to wane that the weight of this tradition could begin to be disregarded. It is easy for any writer on this period to make great play with the stuffy conservatism of those ecclesiastics who tried to appeal to authority and tradition against the new science which threatened their teachings. The appeal to authority has little attraction for us nowadays. However, the issue was not simply whether this or that discovery was to be accepted, or whether this or that tradition was to be vindicated. What was at stake was a whole view of the world, and of man's place in it. Once Aristotle was seriously challenged it could only be a matter of time before the entire structure collapsed, and with it would go the sense that this is God's world made by Him for man. Those who feared the consequences of this collapse had every reason to be alarmed. Never again have men felt so at home in the universe as they felt in the Middle Ages; never again has God seemed so near or so intimately concerned with all the details of life. When we read about some of the extraordinarily silly things which Christians said and did in the early days of modern science, it is as well to remember this.

How and why modern science actually began in the sixteenth and seventeenth centuries is a very complicated story indeed, and I do not intend to go into the details of it. What will concern us in this chapter are some of the ideas and assumptions which accompanied the rise of science, and which were as double-edged as the Greek ideas which went before them.

We saw in the last chapter how science had become fossilised after Aristotle, because he had constructed a system which explained everything, but which was based on far too few facts. With the Renaissance in Europe all that was changed. Men once again became interested in nature for its own sake. They wanted to know facts, they had curiosity, and they believed in their own powers. There was a general stirring of the intellect, and a readiness to break away from tradition.

One of the earliest philosophers of science, Francis Bacon (1561–1626), made it his main point that science could only advance through accumulating facts in large quantities. He believed that all scientists needed to do was to collect and classify facts, and so arrive at general principles; by this method science would infallibly advance, until in a short time the whole structure of nature would be laid bare. Bacon himself was incredibly naïve in his estimate of the amount of facts to be discovered, but his emphasis on them was important. He managed to express something of the spirit of science. Where the choice is between authority and facts, even an authority as venerable as Aristotle's, then facts must have the last word. Nothing is more absurd than the spectacle of eminent ecclesiastics refusing to

look at the satellites of Jupiter through Galileo's telescope because, according to Aristotelian theory, they could not be there.
How could they be? Bodies invisible to the naked eye were of
no use to men, and in a rational world what is useless cannot
exist. So why bother to look? It was against this sort of attitude
that the early scientists had to fight. And Bacon gave them a
useful weapon.

It was a very limited one, however. Science never really
advances far by the method he described. Botany and zoology
are perhaps the best examples of sciences which do. In both of
them a great deal of spade-work has to be done in collecting
and sorting out the various types of living creature. But even
in such relatively simple forms of science, there are mistakes to
be made. There are helpful and misleading ways of classifying
things. The great classifier is not necessarily the man who has
most facts at his fingertips, but the man who has a flair for
seeing how they should be arranged.

Bacon ignored the existence of this kind of flair, and so his
account of the scientific method is curiously unrealistic. A
hundred years before he wrote, Copernicus had given him the
lie.

Everybody knows that Copernicus turned the ancient world
upside down by asserting that the sun rather than the earth was
the centre of the universe. What is not so well known is that he
did it without discovering any new facts. His achievement was
to see the old facts in a new way.

Consider, for a moment, a very simple set of facts, such as the
lines which make up Figure 1. What do they represent? We can

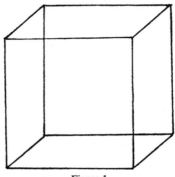

Figure 1

either see a cube looked at from below, or a cube looked at from above, or a wire frame, or just a flat pattern of squares and parallelograms. The facts are the same in each case, but we see them in different ways. So it is with scientific hypotheses. They are not so much classifications of facts as ways of seeing things. As we look at them, suddenly a new pattern seems to click into shape. Then, for a scientist, follows the painstaking business of checking whether the new pattern really fits the facts or not, and if so, what new facts it should lead him to seek.

Ptolemy's model of the universe had held the field since the second century A.D. The idea that the earth might revolve round the sun had been suggested four hundred years earlier by Aristarchus, but nobody took it very seriously. Ptolemy stuck to the commonsense view that the earth is stationary and that the heavens revolve. The main difficulty in this view is that they do not revolve uniformly. The sun, the moon, the stars and the planets all move in relation to one another, as well as revolving once a day round the earth. The planets are particularly awkward because they seem to move backwards and forwards across the sky. Ptolemy explained their motion by the use of a geometrical device known as the epicycle, a circle whose centre moves along the circumference of another circle. By adding

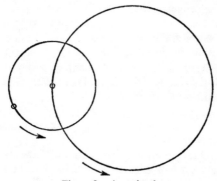

Figure 2.   An epicycle

epicycle to epicycle he was able to work out an incredibly complicated geometrical system, using only circular motion, which fitted the observed movements of the heavenly bodies tolerably well (Figure 2). As time went on the Ptolemaic system had to be modified, and made even more complex, as astronomers made more and more observations.

It was this system which Copernicus proposed to scrap. The only advantage his model had over Ptolemy's was that of simplicity; it relied on the same observations but explained them in a simpler way. The gain in simplicity was not very great. Copernicus was still wedded to the idea of circular motion, which complicated his calculations; but whereas the Ptolemaic system by this time needed eighty circles, Copernicus only needed thirty-four. It was a great act of insight and courage to see that this system did in fact hold more promise for the future than Ptolemy's, despite its unsatisfactoriness. Not only was it not much simpler, but it ran into a difficulty which the old theory never raised. If the earth moves round the sun, then its position should vary throughout the year in relation to the stars; this means that the stars should appear to move in relation to one another, much as a cow seen from a moving train appears to move in relation to some more distant object. But such movements of the stars could not then be observed. The only conclusion possible was that they were an almost infinite distance away. To believe this was to throw overboard the whole Aristotelian conception of the universe as a relatively small-scale affair centred on man, a step which the majority of men, including Copernicus, were not prepared to take. A later astronomer, Bruno, did take it, proclaimed dogmatically that the universe was infinite, and was burnt as a heretic in 1600.

Meanwhile, there were solid reasons why Copernicus's theory should be distrusted. It seemed to conflict with commonsense; it raised all sorts of difficulties about how the earth could revolve without sweeping off everything on its surface, or blowing everything away in a gale; it hinted at greater and more serious changes to follow in man's whole conception of the universe; and all this price was to be paid for a moderate advantage in calculating the movements of the planets. I mentioned earlier the flair which a scientist must have if he is to be more than a mere collector of facts. Copernicus, with his vision of mathematical simplicity, with his readiness to try out a bold hypothesis, and with his persistence in working out its mathematical implications until they fitted the facts, has every right to be called the founder of modern science.

His book *De Revolutionibus Orbium Coelestium* was published in 1543. At first it caused no great stir among theologians, partly because there seemed to be such weighty objections to it, and partly because it was published with a disarming preface by a theologian called Osiander, with whom Copernicus would certainly have disagreed, had he not been already dying when the book came out.

Osiander argued that Copernicus was not describing the universe as it really was, but merely suggesting a mathematical device to simplify calculations about it. Everybody knew that the sun went round the earth. Did not Scripture assume it? How indeed could Joshua have commanded the sun to stand still (Joshua 10: 12) if the sun was standing still already? But if certain mathematicians liked to save themselves trouble by constructing a different model of the universe, that was their business. It did not affect the Truth.

This was enough to allay many fears about the Copernican theory, and even the Pope showed mild interest and approval. Another seventy-three years were to pass before the real crisis came. From about 1610 Galileo had been using the newly-invented telescope to make exciting astronomical discoveries, and in 1613 he published a book on sunspots—a harmless enough subject, one might think, but one which in fact dealt a severe blow to the Aristotelian conception of the universe. What became of the perfection of the heavens if the very sun itself suffered from spots?

Worse was to follow. In 1616 Galileo and the Church came into head-on collision over the interpretation of the Copernican theory. It all began with the discovery of Jupiter's satellites. Galileo argued that if Jupiter could have satellites, so could the sun; by looking through his telescope he had seen a miniature solar system; in other words, he claimed, the Copernican theory was more than a convenient device; it described things as they really were. He supported his argument with other observations which there is no need to bother about here. The important point is that Galileo, by his insistence that the Copernican theory was true in some absolute sense, swept away Osiander's cautions and gave scientific theories a new status. Henceforward science would be concerned with "reality"; it would show the real structure of things. Hitherto scientists had been free to make what theories they liked, because "reality" could only be known by philosophy and theology. But from Galileo onwards science began to invade the Church's own thinking, and conflict was inevitable.

What actually happened has been told often enough in the history books. It will suffice to say that many eminent Churchmen made fools of themselves, and Galileo recanted. But a very deep philosophical problem had been raised about the nature of science, and such problems were not to be settled by appeals to tradition or threats of burning at the stake. We must return to this problem in a moment. Meanwhile there was another side to Galileo's work which we must also note.

Galileo did even more fundamental work in mechanics than he did in astronomy. He realised that the only way to make any progress in the study of motion was to reduce the enormous number of facts to manageable proportions. Rather than speculate about motion in general, he would try to reduce the motion of particular bodies to some sort of mathematical formula. On the practical level, this meant the use of experiment. Measurements of the movements of bodies in general reveal very little of any significance. But comparative measurements of the time taken by balls to roll down inclined planes or to fall from the top of the leaning tower of Pisa, can tell a great deal. The essence of an experiment is so to control conditions and limit the number of factors being studied, that a particular set of facts can be studied in isolation and the result of a particular set of changes can be measured. Experiment, then, is the answer to the problem raised in the last chapter by Aristotle's awareness of the complexity and imperfection of the world. The notion of experiment, too, is one of the missing links in Bacon's conception of science. Bacon was wrong in thinking that facts by themselves are all that science needs; the vital thing in science is to select and study the relevant facts in controlled experiments. And this is what Galileo did.

On the theoretical level, this way of going about his work had extremely important repercussions. We have seen that doing experiments involves making a selection of relevant facts and ignoring others. We have already met this situation in the shape of our mountaineering hippopotamus in the last chapter. The question we must now consider is, how does a scientist decide which facts are relevant and which are not?

There are two answers, a general and a special one. The special one I shall deal with very briefly, since we shall meet it again when we consider the nature of scientific theories. In a word, the answer is that this is the rôle of a good hypothesis. A good hypothesis *suggests* experiments, it suggests that certain ideas are worth testing, certain facts worth looking for.

The general answer to the question must occupy us a bit longer. Galileo answered it by saying that for a scientist the relevant features of any situation are those which can be weighed and measured. Following in Galileo's footsteps we gave the same answer when we considered our hippopotamus sliding down its slope. We ignored its colour, its age, its ancestry, in fact everything which might have made it interesting to another hippopotamus. Instead we concentrated on what we could measure, the angle of the slope, the rate of fall, the weight of the creature.

This is roughly what is meant by the distinction drawn by the English philosopher Locke, between the "primary" and the "secondary" qualities of an object. Weight and size and number are primary qualities; these are the basic features of things, the essence of the "stuff" which makes things what they are. Secondary qualities, on the other hand, exist mainly in our minds; it makes nonsense to talk about the colour, the smell or the feel of an object, unless we think in terms of someone looking or smelling or feeling. This is not to deny that there is something about the basic stuff which makes it look the colour it does. But this sort of quality is less real than the primary qualities; the latter are the basis of everything, including the secondary ones.

Galileo did not philosophise about his discoveries. He simply paved the way for Locke. As a practical scientist he realised that to concentrate on the things he did was the best way to produce scientific results. He wanted to extricate himself from Aristotelian mechanics which were all bound up with obscure ideas about "natural motion" and "impulses" and which, as we have seen, looked for final rather than efficient causes. Weights and measures, on the other hand, were objective things and so were the connections between them. To study them was to study what was really "there"; this was to make science objective; it was to shift the emphasis from final to efficient causality. It was thus a vital part of the birth of science.

Bound up with it was an enormous philosophical assumption, the same assumption which Galileo had made in his astronomy.

The heart of his controversy with the Church was his claim that the Copernican picture of the universe was true in a sense in which the Ptolemaic picture was not. In this he was obviously right. In spite of all sorts of modern difficulties raised by the theory of relativity, it is true to say that the earth goes round the sun and not vice versa, and if we were to go sufficiently far away in a space-ship we should be able to see directly that this is so. However, if we carry over this assumption that science describes "reality" into Galileo's work on mechanics, and into other branches of science, and if in our science we concentrate exclusively on what can be weighed and measured, we end up with a very odd picture of "reality" indeed. "Reality" becomes the world investigated by science, the world of colourless, sound- less, meaningless particles assumed by materialism. This is the origin of the so-called "billiard-ball" conception of the uni- verse, the idea that the whole varied pattern of the world and life can in the end be reduced to descriptions of particles moving about and banging into one another.

Such ideas were a long way in the future when Galileo did his work. Nevertheless the first half of the story of science is the working-out of this kind of assumption, and the roots of the early conflicts between science and religion lie here. On the surface there was a lot of froth and misguided controversy. But underneath there were ideas waiting to bear fruit, which Chris- tians had every reason to fear. There was the loss of a sense of meaning in the universe with the break-up of Aristotelianism. There were new and terrifying perspectives opened up as the immense size of the universe began to become apparent. And there was the hidden assumption that science somehow got to grips with reality in a way which philosophy and theology did not, in fact that the reality described by science was the only reality there was.

The actual controversies took place in a highly charged emo- tional situation in which truth and error were as inextricably mixed as they were in ancient Greece. Philosophers of science still debate the rights and wrongs of Galileo's attitude. In the overthrow of Aristotelianism, in his refusal to consider meaning and final causality as having any place in science, in his con- centration on the mathematical aspects of things, he paved the way for the split between science and culture which everybody is so busy deploring these days. Nevertheless it was this very attitude which enabled science to become objective, and so got it on its feet. He was right in the particular dispute about Copernicus. But was he right as a matter of general principle? Is it true that science shows us what is "really there"?

These are questions to which we shall have to return. Meanwhile science set off along the trail which Galileo had marked out for it, and reached its fulfilment through the genius of Newton.

Chapter 4

THE NEW SYNTHESIS

"Nature and Nature's laws lay hid in night:
God said, Let Newton be! and all was light."

Scientific discovery is a good deal more difficult than this couplet might suggest. Nevertheless, hackneyed though the lines are, they sum up some of the feelings which Newton's discoveries aroused. Men felt that a new era had dawned; it is not for nothing that the age which followed him is known as The Enlightenment.

What did Newton achieve? As before, we shall not be concerned so much with the details of his scientific work, as with some of its implications and the way it was used by those who were not themselves scientists. Science and religion impinge on one another much more on this latter level than on the level of straightforward scientific results.

Surprisingly enough the story of Newton really did begin, as the legend declares, when he watched an apple falling in his garden. It is not true, however, that the apple fell on his head. He had fled from Cambridge in 1665 to escape the plague, and was sitting at home in his mother's garden when the apple started him thinking about the mysterious force which pulls things to the ground; a force which seems to operate everywhere, no matter how high or how low one cares to go. He began to wonder whether the same force might not control even the moon and the planets. In those thoughts were the first glimmerings of a theory which was to unite heaven and earth, which was to show that the heavenly bodies obeyed the same laws as earthly ones, and so was to destroy the last remnants of the Aristotelian conception of the universe.

Newton, of course, built on the work of those who went before him. He brought to their findings a far greater mathematical power than anybody since the days of the great Greek mathematicians; he also had that insight, that ability to frame the right questions, which is the mark of scientific genius. He was a great experimentalist too, but most of his experiments were done in optics. His most famous achievement, the theory of gravitation, was based entirely on observations made by others.

Tycho Brahe (1546–1601) had laid the foundations with a vast number of astronomical observations, the most accurate ever made without the use of telescopes. And Kepler (1571–1630), by vast mathematical labour, had succeeded in reducing these observations to some sort of shape. Kepler was fascinated by mathematics. He was also a deeply religious man who believed that God had written a mathematical riddle into the universe which it was his vocation to solve. And so he worked until he had solved it.

Kepler's laws, published between 1609 and 1619, illustrate very clearly the difference between a brilliant classification and a theory. They show the power and limitations of mathematics. There were three laws:

1. The orbits of the planets are ellipses with the sun at one focus.
2. The line joining any planet to the sun sweeps out equal areas in equal times. (This means that the planets move faster the nearer they approach the sun.)
3. The square of the time taken by any planet to make one orbit round the sun is proportional to the cube of its mean distance from the sun.

What immediately strikes one about these is that they fail to add up to anything coherent. The first is easy to picture, and seems like a fairly straightforward geometrical discovery. For Kepler this was the most difficult law of all to accept, because it involved a change in the way of thinking about the universe; it seemed to him absurd and unworthy that the structure of the heavens should be based on a geometrical figure so imperfect and unsatisfactory as an ellipse. The other two laws, which at first may strike us as interesting but not illuminating, excited Kepler greatly, especially the third one. He was led to it by an analogy with numerical relationships in music; and he found the analogy fitted. Here, then, in a literal sense was the harmony of the heavens revealed. Here was the secret mathematical structure upon which all was based. Here Kepler was content to stop. He had reached a mathematical classification, but not a theory. A different kind of insight was needed before his laws could themselves be explained and related to a larger whole.

Newton's triumph was mainly conceptual. He *thought* about motion in a new way. His basic laws, therefore, are unlike Kepler's in that they are not mathematical, and they are not even based on observations. The laws of motion are abstract; they describe ideal states, i.e. the first law is about what would happen to a moving object which had no external forces acting on it. Such a state has never been achieved in practice; the nearest approach to it is the condition inside a space capsule, described as weightlessness and observed only by the occupants of the capsule. The importance of this first law is that it represents a complete break from older ideas about motion. It arose out of the new ideas about inertia, the recognition that there is something about moving bodies which makes them go on moving long after any obvious external force has ceased to operate. Galileo had wrestled with the idea. Newton crystallised it into the concept of "mass".

The point to note is that this was an entirely new concept; it was a way of expressing the "thinginess" of things, the quality about them which resists us as we try to move them. Henceforward "mass" was to become the fundamental quality of the stuff of which the universe is made. Mass is not the same as weight, since the weight of an object or the pull of the earth upon it varies from place to place. Mass belongs to an object no matter where it is or what it is doing. It seems to tell us about the "real thing".

If now we apply this concept of mass to the planets as they move round the sun we run into a puzzle. Why don't they go on travelling in straight lines? What force is it that bends their orbits and makes them move in ellipses? Can it be the same force which makes the apple fall to the ground? And if so, how must the force vary if the planets are to obey Kepler's laws? These were the questions Newton asked; and, because he was mathematically brilliant enough to tackle the problems of movement in curves, he was able to establish his answer. Bodies attract one another in proportion to the product of their masses, and in inverse proportion to the square of the distance between them. This is the law of gravitation.

It was not only simpler than Kepler's laws; it also explained things in a way which Kepler's laws did not. It was far more than a mere summary of what had been observed; it seemed to provide a model which men's minds could grasp; it made sense of countless phenomena; it could be tested in the laboratory, and applied not only to the planets, but to every particle in the universe. Nobody can understand what science is all about who has not felt the excitement of this kind of discovery. To find fact after fact clicking into place around a successful hypothesis is a deeply moving experience. The theory of gravitation surpassed all that had gone before it in the range of facts to which it could be applied. No wonder Newton became the symbol of an age. Men felt at last that they had solved the riddle of the universe.

Newton's achievement was to establish a new idea of what counts as an explanation. His theory did not explain everything; far from it. He found no satisfactory definition of "mass", and the force of gravity he admitted was a mystery. The very notion of gravitational force raised all sorts of difficulties about how bodies could act upon one another across apparently empty space. This is the famous problem of "action at a distance".

Newton was not unaware of these problems. But he showed his scientific instinct by neglecting them and by using notions which could be expressed quantitatively, even if they could not be understood in any absolute sense. Compared with Aristotle's, Newton's explanations were fragmentary and full of loose ends, wildly incomplete at the most important points. In the Aristotelian sense of the word, Newton did not really "explain" anything. His theory of gravitation related certain concepts to one another, which could be related mathematically—mass, velocity, time, position; the deeper questions it left unresolved.

There was, it must be admitted, another side of Newton which was very interested indeed in these other questions—particularly theological ones. In fact he wrote more theology than he wrote science; but it was very queer stuff, and it is not for this that he is remembered. His science achieved the heights it did precisely because he separated it from these wider questions. In him science at last seemed to have freed itself from dependence on philosophy; it dealt with objective things, masses, moving in an objective space according to mathematical laws. The problems which concerned it, unlike those of philosophy, were ones which could actually be solved.

Couple this picture of scientific explanation with the assumption we met in the last chapter that science reveals to us what is "really there", and it is not surprising to find the philosopher

Hobbes, an older contemporary of Newton, declaring that reality is nothing but "matter in motion". Here, then, we have the beginning of scientific materialism, the billiard-ball universe which we met in the last chapter. Everything is made up of particles which obey mechanical laws; therefore, in principle, everything about the universe can be known, and if it were possible to know the position and velocity of every particle in existence, everything that ever has happened or ever will happen could be predicted. The whole thing is a great machine.

Not many people, of course, took these thoughts to their logical conclusion. Newton himself was not happy that the machine, as he understood it, would work by itself without being thrown off balance. He thought that God must continually correct the irregularities, thereby earning the scorn of those who accused God of inefficiency as a creator. The French scientist Laplace, a hundred years later, showed that the irregularities which worried Newton cancel each other out, and declared in a famous phrase that he did not need God as an hypothesis. It was he who put forward the idea of a completely mechanical, and hence completely predictable, universe in its full rigour.

Such extremism, however, was rare. The usual reaction of these early scientists, most of whom were very religious men, was to marvel at the orderliness of God's creation and the intricate plan which science was revealing.

It was true that science was changing the face of the universe, and that the old sense of intimacy, and the feeling that a miracle might happen at any moment, were being lost. Men knew now the laws by which God operated, and these seemed to allow no possibility of miracle or interference. But the laws themselves were objects of wonder, and opened up new possibilities of worship. The old harmony of the crystal spheres had been broken up, but a new harmony had taken its place. Thus Addison could write at the turn of the seventeenth century:

> "What though in solemn silence all
>   Move round the dark terrestrial ball;
>   What though nor real voice nor sound
>   Amid their radiant orbs be found;
>   In reason's ear they all rejoice,
>   And utter forth a glorious voice;
>   For ever singing as they shine,
>   'The hand that made us is Divine'."

Note the use of the word "real" in line three; the music of the spheres, the singing angels of the mediaeval universe, were no longer "real" in the Newtonian sense. But "reason" (line five) could fill the gap; there was an intellectual music which only an enlightened modern mind could hear.

In such ways many Christians came to terms with what was known as The New Philosophy. But there were others, especially on the Continent, who grasped it as a means of breaking the power of Christianity, which they identified with everything that was authoritarian, obscurantist and reactionary. These men saw science as a means of intellectual liberation. For the most part they were not themselves scientists. Voltaire, one of the most influential of them, was essentially a man of letters. He became interested in physics and wrote a most lucid account of Newton's theories, not because he was concerned about physics as such, but because he saw on a deeper level what Newton had achieved. The theory of gravitation, as was pointed out a moment ago, established a new idea of what counts as an explanation. This vision of a new rational way of understanding things, coupled with the immense practical success of science, intoxicated the thinkers of the Enlightenment. They saw the citadels of ignorance, error and superstition crumbling away before the advance of science. Here was the weapon which could destroy the crippling hold of tradition and authority. It was not the actual scientific theories which excited them so greatly; it was the possibilities of human progress which science seemed to disclose.

It was in many respects a noble vision, even though the early exponents of it made mistakes. But it was a vision, not a scientific discovery. A mechanistic philosophy was accepted, not because science had shown that the universe really is nothing but a great machine, but because this way of looking at things was rational, and held out the best promise of understanding more in the future. As a programme for science the question, "What aspects of nature can be understood in mathematical and mechanical terms" was, and still is, an extremely fruitful one. But as the basis for a world view or a philosophy of life, more is required than the enthusiasm generated by a great scientific discovery.

Imagine for a moment what would have happened if the first great discoveries had been in biology rather than in physics and astronomy. Perhaps it is an unreal speculation, because on the whole it is easier to do controlled experiments in physics than in biology, and physics also lends itself more readily to mathematical treatment. But it is not beyond the bounds of possibility that Darwin's theory of evolution might have been established earlier than Newton's theory of gravitation; Darwin could have reached his conclusions without using any of the findings of physics. If this had happened, then presumably evolution would have become the great model of scientific explanation. Scientists would have tried to explain everything in terms of its development and ancestry. The fundamental categories of science might not be mass, position and velocity, but notions like growth, environment and adaptation.

The philosophers and men of letters might then have drawn their pictures of the universe as a great organism, a swirling sea of change and growth.

Of course, this is fanciful. But at least it makes the point that there was an element of historical accident in the way in which the New Philosophy took the form it did. Newton came first. For good or ill, the picture which gripped men's minds was that of nature as a mechanism; and this was erected into a philosophy, not primarily by the scientists themselves, but by those who popularised their work.

I shall end this chapter by mentioning one of the more unfortunate consequences of all this. Throughout the eighteenth century it was the secret ambition of most social philosophers to do for their own subject what Newton had done for physics. If there was a law which governed the movements of the stars as much as it governed the movements of a falling apple, what reason was there for thinking that man escaped this universal reign of law? What then were the laws by which human society operated? What were the laws governing human nature? If it were possible to lay bare the structure of a society or of a man, as the structure of the physical universe had been exposed, then we should know how we really ought to behave, and how men could live together in peace. Morality, one of the remaining strongholds of religion, would cease to be authoritarian, and would become a branch of applied science.

There, very sketchily, was the ideal of the social philosophers of the eighteenth century. Again, it was a noble ideal; there was truth in it. But as an account of morality or as an approach to the problems of human society it fell disastrously short of the facts.

Since that day sociology and psychology have made enormous advances; it has become increasingly clear, however, that human beings somehow elude that clear, precise, mathematical kind of description which Newtonian physics held up as an ideal; and even if such a description were possible, to understand how human beings function is one thing, and to decide how they ought to behave is another. How men ought to live, the ideals and values which should inspire them, are not things which science by itself can teach us. A mechanistic philosophy, applied miles outside its original context in physics, can narrow down our conception of what it is to be a human being to an absurd degree. And this is what tended to happen in the first flush of excitement which followed Newton.

To pursue this any further would take us too far afield at the moment. I simply use it as an illustration of the final stage of the process I have tried to describe in this chapter. First there comes the great scientific discovery which explains a large number of facts by relating them to each other. Secondly, there is the hold which the theory gets upon the imagination of scientists, so that similar kinds of explanation are sought for other ranges of facts. Thirdly, there is the popular response to the discovery which is then used as the justification for all sorts of ideas, philosophical, political, moral and social, which may have no direct relation at all to the original subject which the discovery was all about. At each stage in this rake's progress philosophical assumptions are made, which may or may not be justified. Even deep in Newton's original theory there were philosophical questions which were ignored. For a time this did not matter; in fact, it was a positive advantage. But philosophy has a way of revenging herself on those who neglect her. Not only the assumptions which were built on it, but Newton's theory itself, were to experience that revenge in the years which followed.

Chapter 5

PROBLEMS OF SPACE

Space is one of those things which we take for granted until somebody starts asking awkward questions. It seems obvious to us that we live in space, and that objects exist in space. We distinguish between different things by the fact that they occupy different spaces. "You can't be in two places at once", we say; and equally, "things must be somewhere."

But what *is* space? Is it a thing at all? Or is it an idea in our minds? And what happens at the edge of space? Is there an edge, or does it just go on and on? And what sense can we make of the notion of empty space? Men have speculated on these questions since they have speculated at all. I mention them here, not because I have an answer to them, but as a reminder that they exist. The notion of space is an oddity. It is one of those unsolved philosophical problems which were mentioned at the end of the last chapter. In this chapter I want to discuss it in a little more detail, to illustrate how philosophy has a habit of worming its way even into what appears to be straightforward science.

The scientific discoveries of the sixteenth and seventeenth centuries brought about tremendous changes in men's conception of space. The Greeks, as might have been expected, had already given a good many of the possible answers to the philosophical problems. But these were not based on any solid evidence, and by the sixteenth century many of them were forgotten. As we have seen, most men, before the scientific revolution, believed that the universe was a relatively small affair; they thought of space as bounded by the heavens above and by the depths beneath. "Space" was the area in between; it was the firmament created by God when He divided the waters from the waters (Genesis 1: 6). This "created space" was not just emptiness. Aristotle had said, "Nature abhors a vacuum"; the notion of empty space seemed to be a contradiction in terms. As we might put it nowadays, they believed that space was filled with matter of varying degrees of "earthiness"; they imagined all sorts of invisible fluids and essences filling every nook and cranny. But to put it like this is unfair to them, because the very notion of space being "full" implies that it might conceivably have been empty; and this is just what they failed to conceive. Most of them had not made our seemingly obvious distinction between matter and space. We tend to think of matter as something existing *in* space; they spoke of matter and space, as it were, in the same breath.

Even a philosopher as modern as Descartes (1596–1650) had not made the distinction, but his contribution to thought about space was so important that we must spend a little time on it.

Descartes was primarily a mathematician, and probably his greatest achievement was his invention of so-called Cartesian Geometry. Everybody who has ever drawn a graph has used Cartesian Geometry. A graph is a way of representing variable quantities geometrically. We draw two lines at right angles to one another, label them as our co-ordinates, and then plot the graph in the space defined by the two lines. Mathematically, this is a process of enormous value and importance. But philosophically, too, it was a big step forward. What Descartes had done was to take this notion of space, a notion so familiar that for most of the time we never think about it, and express it mathematically. Cartesian geometry now became a way of defining space; it became possible to speak precisely of things being in particular places by reference to certain co-ordinates.

There is an obvious application of this principle in geography. The lines of latitude and longitude on an atlas provide us with a sort of grid on which our maps can be drawn. We then no longer have to say "X is fourteen days' journey on a camel from Y". We can say "X is here, and Y is there", and specify on our map precisely where "here" and "there" are. In fact "here" and "there" have become mathematically definable points; there is no need to refer to our different experiences of "X" and "Y" and the long wearisome camel journey between them.

What it is possible to do when mapping the world, it ought to be possible to do when mapping the universe. There ought to be a sort of grid, a set of Cartesian co-ordinates, which applies to the universe as a whole, and which theoretically would enable a super-scientist to say precisely where every particle in it is located. Such was the view of space which Newton took over from Descartes. The Newtonian universe was like a vast three-dimensional billiard table whose edges could never be reached, but whose billiard balls were in particular places in relation to the table.

Of course, the idea of a three-dimensional table without edges is a difficult one to swallow; it is no easier if we call it a box without sides. And we do not need to know much about maps to realise that our lines of latitude and longitude are to a large extent arbitrary. These are difficulties which lurked in the background of Newton's conception of space, and in our own century were eventually to destroy it.

For the present, however, we can ignore them, and explore Descartes' ideas a little further. He believed that the universe consisted of two radically different kinds of substance. For him the most fundamental property of matter was "extension"; in other words, material objects occupy space. All the other properties of matter, like weight and colour and hardness, are secondary; the essential thing is that matter is located somewhere and has particular dimensions. This was the first kind of substance—what he called "extended substance". The second kind of substance existed just as certainly as the first but did not exist in space. It was Thought—or what he called "thinking substance". Thought is the only kind of reality which does not have the property of extension. It is absurd to talk about a thought two feet long or an idea six inches above somebody's head (except in a strip cartoon—but Descartes did not have to contend with those). "Thinking substances" and "extended substances" are completely distinct, and for Descartes were the two kinds of reality of which the world is made.

No doubt we have already spotted that this is roughly the same as our familiar distinction between mind and matter. For making it familiar, almost a piece of mere commonsense, we have to thank Descartes. In his own day the distinction meant a great deal for science; it meant that the whole material world could be handed over to science as the thing which it could study and explain. Here was a world whose fundamental property was extension; therefore mechanics and mathematics were adequate to describe it. The material world, in fact, was nothing but a great machine, and even animals, even the human body, were nothing but machines of enormous complexity.

And all this could be said without treading on the toes of religious belief; indeed Descartes himself was a Christian and wished to defend his faith. Alongside this mechanical material world was the world of thought; this was the realm which distinguished men from machines; this was the realm in which all the things human beings have traditionally prized still had their existence.

This may seem rather a digression from the ideas about space with which we began. But the point is this. To define the fundamental property of matter as extension is to make matter and space identical. For Descartes it was nonsense to talk about two objects as being separated by emptiness. How could there be separation where there was nothing separating things? How could there be extension where there was no matter?

Thus for Descartes the universe was full. It was like the sea where there are no gaps, but only different kinds of material objects. Things influence one another in space as the swirls and eddies in a stream draw objects together and fling them apart. On such a view there can be no problems about "action at a distance". Distant objects may appear to act on one another, only because in fact they are connected.

Such a view is comparatively easy to picture. The trouble is that it is no more than a picture. Swirls and eddies were not the sort of things which in Descartes' day could have been analysed mathematically; and if they could have been, it would have been shown that his picture failed to fit the facts. The future lay with a theory which in some respects was much more difficult to picture, but which was infinitely simpler mathematically. Descartes had asserted as a philosophical principle that the material universe was a machine; Newton revealed its mechanics. He was not concerned to present a picture of how objects could influence one another at a distance; he was content to observe that they did so, and so work out the laws of their interaction. But the type of universe these laws seemed to require was very different from that of Descartes. Whereas for Descartes space and matter were identical, for Newton space was an empty frame which *contained* matter.

The Newtonian universe is the one which most of us now feel fits best with the demands of commonsense. Space and time are the stage on which the drama is played out by matter. Space, time and mass are the three fundamental realities. Space goes on infinitely in every direction; and where there is not matter there is nothing.

For many Christians such a view of the universe seemed hard

to reconcile with the loving care of God for man. The universe began to seem a cold, hard, empty place, with man occupying only a tiny speck in an infinite void. It was true that creation demanded an explanation. There must be a Creator. But all that was needed was someone or something to start the process off, some controlling hand almost infinitely remote. God was pushed further and further into the background, while the great universal machine rolled on its way without Him.

There were other difficulties besides these rather emotional ones. If space was infinite, how could this be reconciled with the infiniteness of God? In the mediaeval picture of the universe, space was finite and God was "outside" it. "Outside" no doubt could be given a very sophisticated interpretation; we are not to think naïvely of God living above the sky. But at least the belief that the universe had an "outside" gave men's imagination something to hold on to. In the new picture there was no "outside"; indeed there was no room for God at all. How could there be two infinites?

Newton played with the idea that space might be one of the attributes of God. Empty space was not a physical reality; it must therefore be spiritual. Objects exist in space, as in some sense they exist "in God". Thus he avoided the problem of the two infinites; the infinity of space, so far from driving God out of the universe, is simply an expression of the fact that "in God everything lives and moves and has its being".

Nevertheless it is difficult to avoid the impression that this is a philosophical muddle. When a theologian talks about the Infinity of God, is it clear that he means by "infinity" what a physicist means when he talks about the infinity of space? One of the most dangerous snares in philosophy is in imagining that the same word always has the same meaning wherever it is used. Likewise one of the big temptations of Christian writers on science is to produce a spurious reconciliation by this sort of easy identification of things which are different.

To find a much more profound approach to the whole problem we must go to one of the greatest of all philosophers, Immanuel Kant (1724–1804). Kant was concerned primarily with the question of how it is that we know things. He is generally thought to be a very difficult philosopher, so that to get across something of his ideas I am going to use an illustration drawn from much later scientific discoveries. Kant's philosophy does not depend on these later discoveries; but they give something of an idea of what he was after.

How do we know things? The physiologist answers that our knowledge of the world comes to us through our sensory nerves. Our sense organs select various kinds of stimuli from our environment—light, sound, touch, heat—and transform these into coded messages, the so-called nerve impulses, which rush along our nerves to our brain. These nerve impulses form a sort of morse code, a pattern of electrical pulses, which are then interpreted by our minds and built up into our picture of the world. But how do we know that this picture corresponds with the world as it really is? We don't. What sort of world should we see if our senses were different, if, for example, we had a sense organ which could detect magnetism? Obviously there are plenty of possible pictures we might have, depending first of all upon our sense organs, and secondly on the way our minds interpret the information they receive.

It was this distinction between the world as it appears to us, and the world as it really is, which was at the heart of Kant's philosophy. He realised that our knowledge of the world is always an interpretation of the information which comes to us. We fit this information into a framework which already exists in our minds. And for him, part of this mental framework was our notion of space.

He pointed out that space is not a thing; it is not something which we can think away and imagine the world without. The notion of space is presupposed in all our thinking about matter. To talk about space, then, is to talk about the way we understand things, not to talk about something which is really there. The real world is unknown, and it is in this realm of the unknown that God encounters us; science deals only with the world of appearance.

At one stroke this seems to resolve our difficulties. We can see how our puzzles about the infinity of space arise from our way of thinking about it. We can see the absurdity of confusing this infinity with the infinity of God. We see how Newton's theories can be absolutely right as a description of our experience of the universe, without in any way conflicting with belief in God.

Yet somehow Kant made his distinctions a bit too rigid. His basic insight, that there is a subjective element in knowledge, a part contributed by ourselves, seems to be unassailable. But can we really believe that there is nothing "in reality" corresponding to our experience of space?

Since Kant's day physics has moved on, and mathematicians have put question marks against the axioms of the old Euclidean geometry, which Newton thought corresponded with the structure of space as it really was, and which Kant thought corresponded with the way our minds work. We shall take up the story again when we consider the theory of relativity. But the essential point to grasp is that physicists now no longer think in terms of one final absolute structure or frame of reference, either in space itself or in our minds. All we can do is to describe things as they appear to us from where we happen to be.

Thus Newton's world picture broke down. But it was not only his idea of space as a sort of fixed scaffolding on which the universe was built, which gave trouble. The nature of gravitation and the problem of action at a distance were awkward philosophical issues which Newton had avoided. But they could not be avoided for ever.

The problem really became acute with the study of electricity and magnetism. One of the first experiments any schoolboy is told to do with a magnet is to plot its magnetic field. He very soon becomes used to this idea of an electric or magnetic "field", a sphere of influence surrounding the particular wire or bar where he thinks of the electricity or magnetism as being located. But what is this if it is not our old friend "action at a distance"? And with the elaboration of a whole new branch of physics, "field physics", the notion of space as mere emptiness filled with little isolated blobs of matter became more and more untenable. Field physics forces us to recognise that the properties of the basic stuff of which the universe is made cannot be concentrated into the minute spaces actually occupied by particles. We have to think of particles as somehow acting through space as a whole.

At first sight this looks like a return to Descartes, for whom space and matter were identical. In a sense it is. But the wheel never turns full circle. In terms of the science of their day, Newton was right and Descartes was wrong. Nevertheless in terms of philosophy, Descartes had tried to tackle problems which Newton had avoided. It has been the whole purpose of this chapter to show that science has in the end been forced to take these problems seriously.

The moral of the story for Christians, if it has one, is to show how dangerous it is to rush prematurely into religious interpretations of scientific theories. Words like "empty" and "infinite", when applied to the universe, seem to carry alarming religious implications. Most of us still feel in our bones that the universe is as Newton described it, and we search in vain for God in the vast empty heavens which seem to mock our insignificance. But these are feelings, not facts. They are our heritage from the time when a particular scientific theory held the field, and seemed to show that the greater part of the universe was mere nothingness, empty alike of substance and of God.

Chapter 6

THEOLOGICAL REACTION

It is not only scientists and philosophers who make mistakes. Theologians are just as liable to do the same, if not more so. Since their mistakes have undoubtedly contributed to the feeling that Christianity is somehow discredited, it is now time to have a look at some of them. But first I must clear up one possible source of confusion. In the period we have so far been considering, many scientists were also concerned with theology, just as many theologians had a deep interest in science. One of the first secretaries of the Royal Society was a bishop, and there is a long list of clergy who have made important scientific discoveries. We have to remember, therefore, that the labels "scientist" and "theologian" do not necessarily refer to different people. Nevertheless I shall use them as convenient ways of describing different kinds of activity: by "scientist" I mean "somebody engaged in scientific work", and by "theologian" I mean "somebody engaged in theological work".

How then did the theologians react? At first, not at all unfavourably. The main opposition to Copernicus and Galileo came from the Roman Catholic church, which had a far bigger vested interest in the Aristotelian picture of the universe than had the Reformers. In fact the Reformation had been partly inspired by the break-up of the old world view, and the desire to get rid of Aristotle and return to the roots of Christianity in the Bible. The two main leaders of thought in the Reformation, Luther and Calvin, were interested in Copernicus's ideas and had no wish to condemn him outright. It is true that they were unconvinced by him, but one can hardly blame them for that in those early years of science, when everything was so uncertain. They did, however, issue a warning against becoming too preoccupied with the study of nature, to the neglect of God. Though there were superficial points at which the new science seemed to conflict with Scripture, as for example in the famous verse about the sun standing still, this did not greatly worry them. In their eyes the key to Scripture was God's revelation of

Himself in Christ, and they were not concerned with incidental pieces of natural history.

Their successors were neither so wise nor so fortunate. By the time Galileo had made his discoveries, and especially by the time of Newton, it was no longer possible to ignore science, nor could reasonable men remain unconvinced by it. Thus the theologians of those days found themselves faced with two main problems:

1. What, if anything, did the new science reveal about God?
2. How did this relate to the traditional basis of Christian belief, the Bible?

We have already seen the answer which some of them gave to the first question. They believed that science was revealing the laws by which God had created the universe. Scientists were "thinking God's thoughts after Him", and thus science could lead only to a deeper understanding of His wisdom, a more reverent contemplation of His mind as reflected in His works. With deeper understanding went greater clarity. Scripture, on the other hand, was obscure and confused. Within recent years Protestants and Catholics had fought their religious wars because they could not agree about how it should be interpreted. Perhaps, it was felt, there was more light to be found in the study of nature than in the difficult and controversial study of the Bible.

Thus began a movement in theology, reaching full force in the eighteenth century, which placed its main emphasis on the revelation of God through nature. What impressed these thinkers most about the great cosmic machine was the skill of its Designer. Over and over again in scientific writings of the time we find exclamations of wonder and delight as the details of the vast intricate plan are exposed. Paley, in the nineteenth century, summed them all up in his famous comment on the structure of the eye, "Even if we had no other example in the world of contrivance except that of the eye, it would be alone sufficient to support the conclusion that we draw from it, as to the necessity of an intelligent Creator."

The answer of such men to the second question, How does all this relate to the Bible? follows fairly straightforwardly from their answer to the first. Where nature is clear as a revelation of God, and Scripture is obscure, Scripture must be clarified in the light of reason. If Scripture speaks of things which science has shown are contrary to its laws, then Scripture is wrong. To put it crudely, miracles cannot happen; therefore if the Bible contains miracle stories, this does no more than expose the credulity or dishonesty of those who wrote it. Likewise, where the Bible speaks of mysteries beyond our understanding, or where it appears to contain contradictions, these are no more than evidence of confusion or deliberate mystification. Reduced to its essentials the Bible contains only instructions about the right kind of moral life and rational worship. What it says must be passed through the sieve of reason, and all its complexities smoothed out.

This is probably a rather more radical answer to the question than most men would have given, though some eighteenth century thinkers certainly wrote in these terms. What is obvious to us nowadays is how easily this kind of answer allows the content of the Christian faith to dwindle away until eventually there is nothing left. Those who thought in this way found that God, as known through nature, became more and more shadowy and remote as science advanced; and God, as revealed in Scripture, had no power to correct the balance since Scripture itself was regarded as being only of secondary importance.

There were others, probably the majority, who saw the dangers in this reduction of Christian truth to what could be shown to fit with the discoveries of science. They realised that what the Bible tells us about God and man is the very centre of the Christian faith and cannot be pushed on one side. God can only be known through what He has revealed of Himself, and revealed supremely in Christ. He is not part of a scientific hypothesis; He is not an extra and odd variety of explanation dragged in when scientific explanation comes to an end. There are some things we can know by studying nature, and there are other things we can know by studying God's acts in history, and especially that bit of history which finds its climax in the coming of Christ. Thus the answers which these theologians might have given to our two questions were:

1. Science does not tell us very much about God.
2. The Bible is concerned with a different kind of truth, the truth which we learn through God's revelation of Himself in Christ.

Unfortunately this was not the way they put it. They felt, justifiably, that the Bible speaks to us with a peculiar authority about God. They believed that in matters of theology it should come first, not second. But what they failed to see was the many-sidedness of the notion of truth. They wanted to assert that God has truly revealed Himself in the Bible. What they found themselves saying was that the Bible was true; and when pressed to make clear what they meant by "true", they went on to define it as "accurate literally and historically".

If the Bible is the word of God, they argued, it must be perfect. Every book, every sentence, every syllable must have been dictated by God, and must mean exactly what it says. Where Scripture seems to speak about historical events, these must have happened exactly as they are described. Where it tells the story of creation, this is in literal fact the way in which the world was made.

In support of these claims they appealed mainly to miracles and to prophecy. Miracles, to them, were evidence of a supernatural order; they were interruptions in the normal course of things which showed the sovereignty of God over His creation. Prophecy was the guarantee of His sovereignty over time. The fact that the Old Testament contained prophecies which were fulfilled in the New Testament was proof that this was no ordinary book, nor were these merely normal events. Here was scientific evidence, they said, that the Bible is the inspired word of God.

The same argument is still sometimes used today. In one of the American Fact and Faith films, issued during the 1950s, the audience is invited to believe in the Bible on the grounds that the prophecy of the destruction of Tyre in Ezekiel chapter 26 has been literally fulfilled, even in spite of the fact that there is a flourishing modern city where Tyre used to be.

There is little excuse for such a line of argument in the twentieth century. Though Christians have always placed great emphasis on miracles and prophecy, this kind of quasi-scientific interpretation of them, which flourished in the period we are considering, was a mistake, and ought to be acknowledged as such. In the early church they were assessed quite differently. Because the first Christians were convinced that Jesus was the Messiah, the Coming One, the fulfilment of men's hopes and longings, so they searched the Scriptures and found that passage after passage took on a new meaning in the light of what Jesus had done. And because His coming was, as they believed, the supreme act of God in revealing Himself and bringing salvation to the world, so it was fitting that it should be accompanied by signs or miracles, which demonstrated on a smaller scale the work which He had come to do. Prophecies and miracles were not pieces of scientific evidence which proved the truth of the claims of Jesus; they were the pointers which faith could follow as it tried to respond to Him.

What went wrong in the seventeenth and eighteenth centuries was that a conception of truth was taken over by theologians from natural science, and applied inappropriately to their own subject-matter, and in particular to the Bible. The notion of literal and historical truth is not one demanded by the Bible itself; in fact it is foreign to the whole thought-world of Biblical times. It is much more nearly related to the world of Galileo and Locke and those thinkers who believed that science was revealing the "real" nature of things, and that truth was ultimately reducible to clear and distinct ideas. Locke himself stated that the existence of God could be known "with mathematical certainty", a remark which he intended as a compliment to theology. The ideal basis of Christian belief would be for him something like a geometrical proof.

In this prevailing atmosphere, it is easy to see how theologians made their mistakes. On the one hand they wanted to assert the uniqueness of revelation; but on the other hand they were tempted to do so in terms which, at a far deeper level, involved a hidden surrender to science. Thus it was, as the years went by, that conservative theologians found themselves defending more and more impossible positions. To treat Scripture as if it were an alternative source of scientific knowledge, and then to pit it against scientific discoveries, is to invite defeat every time.

In fairness to these theologians it ought to be added that they thought they were simply upholding the traditional view of Scripture, and were not themselves conscious of the assumptions they were making. For centuries the Bible had been accepted in a completely uncritical spirit, and there had seemed to be no good grounds for adopting any other attitude. In the first encounters between Christianity and Greek intellectualism problems had been raised about the historical accuracy of certain parts of the Old Testament, and a third century theologian like Origen had found no difficulty in saying that they were not to be taken literally. "What man of sense," he wrote, "will suppose that the first and second and third day, and the evening and morning, existed without a sun and moon and stars? Or that God walked in a garden in the evening, and that Adam hid himself under a tree! Or that the devil took Jesus into a high mountain, when He could see the Kingdoms of the Persians and Scythians and Indians?" It was plain to Origen that Scripture must have many levels of meaning. But by the seventeenth century all this was ignored. Tradition seemed to demand uncompromising acceptance of precisely what was written. And for Protestant theologians the situation was made even more difficult by the need to find some infallible authority to set against the claims of Rome. If Scripture was the rule of faith for Protestants, how could it give clear guidance unless it was taken at its exact face value?

We may reflect wryly, in the light of subsequent Christian divisions, that even the literal interpretation of Scripture is not unambiguous. But be that as it may, these were some of the forces leading to that head-on collision between science and conservative Christianity which took place in its most dramatic form in the nineteenth century. Matthew Arnold, writing in the latter half of the century, caught a little of the tragedy of it in his phrase, "where ignorant armies clash by night".

Nevertheless, misunderstanding and mistaken assumption are not the whole of the story; nor can we claim that Matthew Arnold's "night" is wholly past. We have seen the danger of treating all truth as if it were scientific truth, and therefore of trying to defend the notion of revealed truth by making absurd scientific claims. But if revealed truth is not like scientific truth, what is it? In fact, what do we mean by truth at all?

Some theologians have come to the opposite extreme from the conservatives we have so far been considering, and have spoken of theological truth as primarily poetic, evocative, a set of symbols which gives us the right feeling towards the world and a sense of the presence of God. Schleiermacher (1768–1834) began a new movement in theology by his definition of religion as "a feeling of absolute dependence". Here "feeling" is intended to mean not simply an emotional attitude, but a new level of awareness, the sort of knowledge of ourselves that we can have as finite creatures confronted with overwhelming mystery.

In an age when it was all too easy to regard the knowledge of God's workings as if it was on the same level as the knowledge of the working of a steam engine, this insight of Schleiermacher's was extremely important, and injected new life into theology. Religious truth is not something which we can learn from textbooks, not even from the Bible as if it was a sort of inspired textbook; nor is it a set of formulae or statements about the nature of reality, which we simply have to accept, like the statement that the world is spherical. It is much more like a man's knowledge of himself, the insight which he gains when he is prepared to contemplate the depth of his experience, to humble himself, and to commit himself to a course of action. So Coleridge, an almost exact contemporary of Schleiermacher, could write of the Bible, "whatever *finds* me bears witness for itself that it has proceeded from a Holy Spirit. . . ." This is another way of making the point that religious truth is what is true *for me*; it is what grasps me, and changes my life.

But to express it like this is already to show up the weakness of such a view. In reacting against a quasi-scientific notion of religious truth, Schleiermacher, and more particularly his followers, fell into the trap of making religion purely subjective. The Christian faith claims to tell us about God and the world, not merely about the state of our own feelings. Christians have worshipped Jesus Christ because they have believed that He was the revelation of God, and as such died and rose from the dead. So they are forced to ask questions like "In what sense is the resurrection a scientific fact, open to the ordinary methods of scientific and historical investigation?" and "How far does the belief that the Bible is more than poetry, and really tells us about the acts of God, involve the acceptance of it as literally and historically true?" Clearly the relation between the Christian faith and scientific and historical truths is more complex than anything we have yet described. We shall be returning to it in a later chapter. Meanwhile, we are in a position to reject three false solutions. There can be no lasting reconciliation between science and theology either by allowing science to dictate the terms in which the Bible must be interpreted, or in Biblical literalism, or by removing theology altogether from the sphere of scientific investigation and trying to find a precarious place for it in the realm of feeling. All these points of view have their representatives today, and all contain, as I have tried to suggest, half-truths. It is often the very element of truth in a half-truth which encourages it to harden into a cantankerous dogmatism.

Chapter 7

LIFE

What is the difference between a screaming animal and a squeaking machine? Apart from obvious differences in the way in which the noise is produced, Descartes would probably have answered, none. As we have already seen (Chapter 5), for Descartes animals were machines and nothing more. He did not believe this because he was hard-hearted or had never watched how animals behave, but because he started from a philosophical idea, the rigid distinction between thought and matter. Everything which belonged to the material world, he believed, could be explained in terms of mechanics. Only thought did not obey the laws of mechanics, and only human beings could think because only they had reason and language. Animals unfortunately came on the wrong side of the line; therefore they were machines.

Descartes appealed to scientific evidence to support his conclusion. William Harvey, in England, had recently demonstrated the circulation of the blood. Here then was proof that one of the most vital systems in the animal body operated according to the ordinary laws of hydraulics. The programme confronting biologists was clear; they must investigate and explain the immensely complicated machinery of which the body is made, and demonstrate how it all works in terms of the known laws of physics and chemistry.

In that last sentence I have taken the liberty of using slightly more modern terms than would have occurred to Descartes. When he wrote about machines he had in mind relatively crude machines like clocks and dancing dolls; he thought of levers and joints and strings. But the principle remains the same if, instead of talking about mechanics, we talk about physics and chemistry. His claim was that there is no essential difference between the study of animals or the human body, and the study of the material world.

Not many people were at first prepared to agree with him. It is true that the spell of Newtonian physics lay heavily upon people's imaginations. The ideal kind of explanation was the kind which Newton had shown was able to unite the study of heaven and earth. But there is something about living things which will not allow us to reduce them wholly to mechanical systems. There must, it seems, be something extra, some vital principle or spark of life, which makes the difference between a living body and a dead one. The reactions of living creatures are so varied, so well adapted to their environment, so super-ficially unlike those of non-living things, that only very strong theoretical considerations could make anyone believe otherwise. And in the early days of biology such considerations did not exist. Descartes' mechanistic approach seemed to raise more problems than it solved.

Thus began the so-called mechanist-vitalist controversy. Throughout its history the opposition to Descartes' views has taken, and still takes, many forms. There have been crude, and now discredited, theories of "vital spirits". There have been more subtle attempts to draw attention to the organising powers of living things. An animal, we are told, is not merely a collec-tion of physical and chemical reactions; it is a highly organized system; and therefore in any account of it we fail utterly if we ignore its organisation, or, as some would put it, if we fail to treat it as an organism. We have to pay attention to the animal as a whole, and hence to those forces which make it operate as a whole. Some parts of it, like the circulatory system, or any other system which the physiologists can isolate and explore, may be explained in ordinary scientific terms; but it is impos-sible to understand the whole in such terms. There remains something extra which physics and chemistry cannot grasp.

Such thoughts find an echo in the fear, which many people feel, that if ever scientists succeed in synthesising a living system in the laboratory, a severe blow will have been struck at re-ligion; our reverence for the mystery of life will be disastrously weakened. People must have felt the same fear when chemists first synthesised one of the simplest chemicals found in living things—urea; the gap between organic and inorganic chemistry was crossed; life was brought one step nearer recognition as no more than a complicated version of things which were already understood. Or again, the discovery of viruses, and the in-ability of scientists to decide whether to call them living or non-living, seems to constitute a threat even to our attempts to define what we mean by life. That such discoveries should arouse anxiety, unnecessary anxiety as I hope to show later, is a sign that most of us feel very deeply that physics and chemistry are not enough to explain life. Vitalism tries to express this feeling scientifically. Many of the positive forms it has taken may seem faintly absurd to us now. But we miss the point of it unless we see that basically it is a negative protest, an expostulation that physicists and chemists ought not to be allowed to have it all their own way.

One of the most famous critics of physics and chemistry was Goethe (1749–1832), and it is no coincidence that he was also one of the last of the "whole men", one of those men whose interests and whose expert knowledge extended everywhere, before we all became divided up into our little specialities, physicists, biologists, poets, theologians and what not. Goethe is chiefly remembered nowadays as a poet, but in his own day, and still to some extent in Germany, he was reverenced as a scientist; and he himself regarded his scientific work more highly than anything else he did. He criticised Newton and his followers for dividing up the things they studied; for concerning themselves with bits and pieces rather than with the whole. Newton, with his prism, analysed light into corpuscles, which were then claimed to be "the real thing". Goethe would contemplate light and colour directly; the reality of it was what we experience when we let Nature speak for herself. A biologist inspired by Newton would dissect a living plant and try to find the secret of its life in the fragments. Goethe would see its life and growth as a whole, and would try to enter sympathetically into the cycle of its life as it was being itself. He and his followers have claimed that genuine scientific laws of growth and development have been discovered by this sort of sympathetic awareness. And there are still those, though they are few today, who believe that science took a wrong turning when it rejected Goethe's concern with the wholeness of things.

The trouble is that it is so difficult to put this kind of insight into precise words. It is much easier to understand a less radical position, which would recognise the importance of physics and chemistry in their proper spheres, but would insist that biology is a distinct science with its own special types of explanation.

In Chapter 2 we saw how Aristotle was concerned to explain things in terms of their purposes, and how this sort of explanation has considerable uses in biology. "The purpose of the heart is to pump blood round the body" tells us a biological truth. Whereas a remark like "the purpose of the hardness of iron is to enable it to be used for making tools" tell us something about human beings, but nothing at all about physics. Here, then, is an obvious difference. But is it a fundamental one? Again, biologists have their own vocabulary; they use words like "adaptation", "co-ordination", "response" which have no place in physics. Does this then mean that biology is fundamentally different from physics, and cannot be reduced to it? Those who answer yes are trying to defend in modern terms what vitalism has always stood for, even though they may reject all the older vitalistic theories.

I hope this makes it clear that vitalism is not one particular theory which can be accepted or rejected as it stands, but rather a persistent feeling of uneasiness about an approach to biology which would seem to empty it of special significance.

The case for mechanism is much easier to put. Like vitalism, mechanism is not one particular theory. Nobody in their senses now believes that animals are machines, as Descartes seems to have believed. All that the modern mechanist would claim is that in the end physics and chemistry will be sufficient to explain the phenomena of life, even if in the process they themselves have to be modified. Physics has undergone some startling changes already in this century, and there may be more to come. But, according to the mechanist view, such changes would not alter the fact that the physical processes, which undoubtedly form the basis of life, must ultimately be capable of explanation in physical terms. What must be absolutely rejected is the notion that at a certain point in the study of living things one comes upon a mysterious something which no longer obeys any recognisable physical or chemical laws. To believe that this might happen is to retreat into mystery and to put a stop to science.

Supporters of this view will point out how barren, in fact, vitalistic theories have been. A "vital principle" which is not sharply defined and cannot be submitted to ordinary scientific tests, explains nothing. Furthermore, modern biologists try to avoid the language about purpose which Aristotle would have approved. Rather than speak, for instance, about a salmon "trying to reach the sea" during the migration season, they would talk in terms of its glandular reactions to changes in the length of the day; these in turn lead to increasing restlessness which results in the salmon being carried downstream. There is an appearance of purposive behaviour, but scientific understanding only begins when this is ignored and the underlying causes are found.

Even special biological concepts like "adaptation", "co-ordination", etc., do not demand a special status for biology. With the growth of mechanical and electronic control systems most of the things which animals do can, at least in theory, be paralleled by the behaviour of machines. It makes perfect sense to speak of a guided missile adapting its behaviour to follow a moving target, and nobody supposes that it obeys anything but the laws of physics and chemistry.

"I entirely agree," a vitalist might reply at this point, "but your argument overlooks the fact that the missile has been built by a human being who knew what he was doing, and why. Of course it obeys the laws of physics and chemistry. But it also acts in a purposive way because purpose has been built into it. It is impossible to understand it completely in terms of ordinary physico-chemical principles because these ignore the most important fact about it, namely that it is organised in a particular way."

So the argument might continue. But by now I hope it will be clear that it is the sort of argument which could go on indefinitely, because the mechanist and vitalist are in fact talking about different sides of the same thing. The mechanist is right when he insists that life is a physico-chemical process, which must therefore be capable of being explained in physico-chemical terms. The vitalist is right when he claims that life has a special status, given to it by the fact that we are ourselves alive. We know what life is, as it were, from the inside; and therefore we feel dissatisfied when we are told that it is nothing but a matter of physics and chemistry. Both are wrong when they argue about whether or not some extra factor or organising principle is "really there". It is the same kind of mistake we met in Chapter 3; we saw there the danger of passing too easily from some particular scientific discoveries, like Galileo's, to generalisations about the nature of reality. Physicists and chemists are concerned with the behaviour of atoms and molecules, and are tempted to think of reality in terms of these

Their opponents have too often started from the same assumptions, and have then found themselves asserting the existence of a mysterious something which physics and chemistry cannot detect.

The whole controversy illustrates the importance of asking the right questions. Questions of the form, "Here is a mechanical system; does it contain anything more, and if so where does it fit?" lead, as we have seen, to hopeless confusion. A more profitable kind of question, I suggest, would be of the form "What are the most useful terms in which to try to understand living creatures?" This immediately suggests the further question "Useful for what?", to which more than one answer is possible. Thus we find ourselves with a series of answers to the first question, which take account of the fact that it is possible to look at life from more than one point of view. The approach has the advantage of starting from living things as we actually know them, rather than from philosophical assumptions about the nature of reality.

Suppose we want to try to understand the circulation of the blood; we soon discover that the most useful terms are purely mechanical ones; and when we have described it in such terms we feel we have all the explanation we need. In the study of nervous conduction, the most useful terms were first found to be electrical; a nerve impulse was described as an electrical change propagated along a nerve at a certain fixed velocity. More recent research on nervous conduction has tried to describe the process in chemical terms, as an example of ion exchange across a semi-permeable membrane.

The brain as a whole is much too complicated to be discussed in such terms as these. Electrical and chemical changes take place in it, and the study of them provides important clues about the way it functions. Therefore at a certain level of understanding, questions about the chemistry of the brain have their uses; but they do not take us very far in understanding how it functions *as a brain*. Explanations in terms of communication theory, using the analogy of a factory or computer in which large quantities of information are stored and exchanged, are more promising. And the same type of theory will probably become increasingly useful in the study of the single living cell. We shall have to return to problems about the brain in a later chapter. At the moment I am simply using it as an example of a system where different kinds of question have different degrees of usefulness.

What is true of the brain is even more true of a complete living creature. We can ask physical and chemical questions about its heat exchange, its metabolism, its chemical constitution, and these answers provide useful information, helping us to understand its feeding habits, why it is generally found in a certain climate, and so on. We can ask more complicated questions about behaviour patterns, as in the case of a migrating salmon, and understand these in terms of a sensitive system reacting to changes in its environment. But what is it to understand an animal *as a living creature*? I believe it means to recognise that it has a certain kinship with ourselves; that we belong to the same family.

In understanding another human being, this sense of kinship is essential. In fact, in ordinary language, to "understand" a person is to have a sympathetic awareness of him, to feel for him, rather than to have a knowledge of his internal workings. As we move down the animal scale, the sense of living contact becomes more and more remote, and the value of sympathetic awareness becomes more questionable. Most people, I believe, would agree that it is only possible to understand a dog if one to some extent feels for it, and thinks of it as having a personality, extremely rudimentary maybe, but not wholly unlike one's own. Whereas even though one may call an old motor car Geneviève, and talk about it affectionately as having a personality, this is of no use whatever in understanding it when it goes wrong. So far the difference between living and non-living creatures seems plain enough.

But what about bacteria? In what sense can it be useful to think of these as having a kinship with ourselves? Clearly such talk has very little use indeed, and any descriptions of bacterial behaviour which relied on human analogies, which spoke of bacteria "trying" to do this or that, would be completely worthless. Yet the fact remains that we are related to bacteria in a way in which we are not related to mere physical objects. They have potentialities and powers of response which we can recognise as being developed to the nth degree in ourselves. In trying to understand the bacteria themselves, it probably does not matter very much whether we use the word "life" or not. But when we ask about their place in the scheme of things, when we try to describe the different kinds of things there are in the world, we are, I believe, saying something significant about them when we say that they are alive, even though we have not been able to define precisely what we mean by life.

This may seem a very nebulous conclusion; but I hope that at least it has illustrated the way in which apparently insoluble problems about the nature of life can be made to look less formidable by adopting a rather different approach to them. Theologians have been involved in these controversies, because in the days when science seemed to be showing that the universe was nothing but a vast machine, to concentrate on the uniqueness of living things seemed to be a way of escape from materialism. As has so often happened in the history of the relation between science and theology, a right instinct led to a wrong reaction, and the result has been a persistent nervousness in Christian circles about what the scientists will disclose next concerning the mystery of life.

That very phrase "the mystery of life" is a good example of the confusions which have surrounded the subject. To scientists life is mysterious because it is an extremely complicated phenomenon whose physico-chemical basis has not yet been unravelled. But this is the kind of mystery which science progressively clears up. For Christians, and indeed for any human being not at that moment engaged in doing science, "the mystery of life" refers to the strange and wonderful experience of being alive. No amount of scientific understanding of the basis of life makes this experience any less significant or inexpressible. It is something we know by direct awareness, and so cannot be affected one way or the other by scientific investigation. Conflict between these two points of view can only arise when we ask questions about the value of this awareness of life from the inside, in the study of biology. It seems to me that there is a certain tendency among scientists merely to be content with physico-chemical questions, and not to recognise how much our understanding of life as a scientific phenomenon secretly depends on our own inner experience of it.

Chapter 8

NOTHING BUT APES ?

When people talk of conflict between science and religion almost automatically they think first of the nineteenth century controversy over evolution. The conventional picture of those days shows scientists and theologians in sharp opposition, the scientists ruthlessly putting man in his place as one among the animals, the theologians desperately appealing to human dignity and the authority of Scripture. From the theologian's point of view, so it seemed, the collapse of the so-called Scriptural account of the origin of species, the doctrine of special creation, was bad enough; what was infinitely worse was the removal of any special mystery surrounding the origin of man himself; the last piece of evidence proving the handiwork of God in nature seemed to have been destroyed.

The last-ditch mentality of both scientists and theologians undoubtedly made the controversy more bitter than it might have been; there were some who then believed, and a small minority who still do, that evolution and Christianity are incompatible. The story goes that a group of Christians was once heard to pray: "O Lord, don't let this evolution be true; and if it is, then don't let it be generally known." But if there were Christians who were afraid to face the facts, on the other side there were also unbelievers who deliberately used the theory of evolution as a stick to beat the faithful with, even though their own rejection of Christianity had quite different and more personal roots. Darwin lost his faith because he could no longer stomach the crude doctrines of atonement and hell which were current in his day. His theory of evolution simply confirmed him in his unbelief; it was not the cause of it. And the same is true of many of the famous Victorian doubters.

The fact is that the issues at stake in these controversies were much more subtle than can be expressed in any conventional picture of scientific enlightenment versus theological prejudice. By now in this book, we should be used to this sort of cautionary remark. In any controversy there are those who adopt extreme and untenable positions, and make fools of themselves; this happened in generous measure in the nineteenth century. Perhaps more eminent Christians, at least in England, made fools of themselves than at any other time. But it is worth recording that there were also theologians (notably Dr. Hort of Cambridge) who saw straight away the importance of Darwin's theory, and accepted it gladly; and there were scientists who, for what seemed then to be good scientific reasons, rejected it. If the majority of theologians had been less closely tied to a literal interpretation of the Bible, and if some scientists had been rather less sweeping in their claims about evolution, most of the controversy could have been avoided. Most, but not all.

The actual course of events has been described many times, and so there is no need to retell the story here. I want to concentrate instead on the larger issues. First, what was Darwin's achievement? Secondly, what, if any, were the genuine reasons for theological anxiety?

It has been said that Darwin did for biology what Newton did for physics. He provided a framework into which an immense number of biological observations could be fitted; and he gave biology a new model of what counts as an explanation. The idea of evolution had been in the air a long time before the *Origin of the Species* was published in 1859. Darwin's achievement was to link it to the concept of natural selection, as the mechanism by which changes in biological make-up could be used and stabilised, and to show that this mechanism was, in a great many different examples, sufficient to account for the facts. I have deliberately used the word "mechanism". The theory completely avoided talk about purpose, life forces and all the rest of the vitalistic language we met in the last chapter. Though Darwin himself did not go far in this direction, it was he who made it ultimately possible for biologists to use mathematical explanations. The modern evolutionist, with the knowledge of the mechanism of heredity which was denied Darwin, can make an assessment of the probabilities of evolutionary change, and show that evolution is mathematically feasible according to the laws of statistics. To be able to do this is to put biology almost on a level with physics, and it is in this sense that Darwin paved the way for a new type of biological explanation.

To say this is not, of course, to surrender to a mechanistic view of life. It is simply a further working-out of the principles discussed in the last chapter. But it raised, and still raises, theological problems.

The most urgent of these concerned the notion of providence. There is always a tendency among Christians to think of God's activity in the world as being confined to the processes which are not understood. The origin of life is a puzzle; the bewildering variety of animals and plants cries out for explanation; the early history of man is largely unknown; the difference between men and animals seems, from certain points of view, to form an unbridgeable gulf. These gaps in our knowledge have provided tempting opportunities for religious people to say, "Aha, here we must talk about a special act of God." When science then begins to close the gaps, the result has too often been religious bewilderment and alarm, the feeling that God has been shown to be unnecessary. Even if it is still claimed that He is necessary in some ultimate sense, the feeling remains that He has been pushed one step further away from any real concern with the affairs of the world.

Darwin's theory at first produced precisely this feeling. If evolution was a process which went inexorably on its way and could account for the variety of living creatures by the operation of a mechanistic law, in what sense was it still possible to believe in God's providence or to think of Him as the Creator? Worse still, one of the most popular arguments for the existence of God had been the apparent design in nature which could only be explained by believing in a Designer. The theory of evolution seemed to shatter this argument; the wonderful adaptation of living things to their environment and to each other, so far from being evidence of a Master Mind, was accounted for by the fact that only those creatures which adapted themselves successfully managed to survive.

It was not long before theologians began to counter these feelings by talking about evolution as God's way of creating. All science had done was to reveal the processes through which God was at work. God works through natural laws, not in spite of them; therefore no amount of explanation in terms of natural laws can make anything less truly the handiwork of God. Indeed there were soon seen to be theological advantages in Darwin's theories as against the doctrine of special creation. The latter implies that God has only created at certain moments and in certain places; whereas evolution presupposes that God is continually active, and that there is never a moment in which it makes sense to think of Him as absent.

Even the argument for God's existence from the apparent design in nature, was shown not to have been so fatally wounded as was feared at first. The real basis of the argument is not that this or that animal fits perfectly into its environment, but that nature is rational, that it makes some sort of sense. And this, as we saw in Chapter 2, is something which men must believe before they can even begin to be scientists, and therefore it is a belief which no amount of scientific discovery can possibly destroy. In fact, the more science makes sense of things, the more firmly we ought to believe that the reality behind nature is a mind not unlike our own.

Important though they are, such arguments do not have the same direct appeal as the older ones; and even if they are accepted, there remain some awkward questions. A God who works through natural laws feels much more remote than a God whose special acts of creation and whose interventions are obvious for all to see. And there is a difficulty too, about the *kind* of laws through which evolution is said to operate. Is it fitting that God should create through an apparently blind process dependent on chance—a process which demands a life and death struggle between His creatures?

I do not believe these questions can yet be answered entirely satisfactorily, but their awkwardness has been eased considerably since Victorian theologians puzzled over them. As so often happens, the easement has come through the advance of science itself. Many biologists are now beginning to stress that evolution is far less mechanical a process than it seemed to be in the first flush of discovery. In the days when physicists thought primarily in terms of little hard billiard ball-like atoms and the mechanical forces between them, it was natural for biologists to wish for the same simplicity; hence we find accounts of evolution which treat animals merely as if they were physical objects in competition with one another. In a later stage of evolutionary theory all the emphasis was on the evolution of germ cells or genetic material, as if the body which grew from those cells were comparatively irrelevant. But this is altogether too narrow a view. In recent years it has been realised that whether an animal survives or not depends on its behaviour as well as on its physical make-up. C. H. Waddington even writes about animals "choosing their environments" and gives this an important place in his account of evolution. To put it in more general terms, the rôle of consciousness cannot be irrelevant in evolution, otherwise conscious creatures would never have evolved; and they undoubtedly have, or you would not be reading this book. But if consciousness plays a real part in the process, and if the end products are conscious creatures capable of understanding their own development, in what sense can the whole process be called blind?

There have been attempts to rewrite the story of evolution, stressing this conscious side of it. One of the most popular of them, *The Phenomenon of Man* by Teilhard de Chardin, described itself as the story of the evolution of consciousness written from within. By taking the fact of consciousness seriously, he claimed to be able to show that the process, far from being blind, is profoundly meaningful; it reaches its climax in the emergence of consciousness in man, and in his possibilities of response to God. Some scientists have been scathing about this account; but at least the point has been made that a religious view of evolution can be more than a set of platitudes, and can draw attention to facts which are largely ignored in other accounts. Whatever the final verdict on Teilhard de Chardin, he has shown that to talk about evolution merely in terms of "blind chance" begs just as many questions as to talk about it as an act of God.

But what of the method of evolution? Here again, we can note that modern biologists talk less about the "struggle for existence" and "nature red in tooth and claw" than did their forefathers. Animals and plants do not merely compete with and kill one another; they also depend on one another and co-operate with one another. Is it more natural to talk about a cow struggling against the grass in the fight for life, or about a cow depending on grass? Surely both kinds of language have their uses when we want to make different points about the cow-grass relationship; the former when we want to describe the forces which control the spread of grass, the latter when we are thinking about the internal economy of cows. Both kinds can be misleading when we read our own feelings into them and try to make out that the universe is either a charnel-house or an immense and beautiful harmony.

We are not in a position to say whether God could or ought

to have devised some different method of bringing us all into existence. All we know is that the universe seems to be a mixture between good and evil, beauty and pain, and that suffering is at least one of the instruments used in the process of creation. The only people who need be disturbed by this are those who believe that our sole source of values and the sole basis for any sort of religion is nature itself. This explains why some of the most persistent objectors to the theory of evolution have not been Christians, but various kinds of post-Christian moralists, like Bernard Shaw, who wanted to retain Christian values without Christian doctrine. Christians themselves, on the other hand, have always believed in the love of God because He has revealed Himself as Love in Jesus Christ, not because they have found that on the whole the universe points to the value of love, rather than vice versa. Furthermore, they should hardly be surprised to find suffering being used creatively in God's world, when the central symbol of their faith is the Cross.

I do not pretend that these thoughts clear up all the difficulties. It is part of the main thesis of this book that there is always a tension between the scientific and the religious ways of looking at things. But a great deal of the tension, where evolution is concerned, seems to have had two unnecessary causes. First, the theory was put forward at a time when Christians were still hoping to find evidence of God's activity in the gaps in scientific knowledge; and Darwin's closure of this particular gap seemed like the last straw. Secondly, the language used by evolutionary enthusiasts, and the tendency to read all sorts of moral implications into the facts of nature, seemed to suggest that the universe was a cruel and heartless place, unworthy to be called the creation of a loving God.

There were, however, still further grounds for theological anxiety—and more valid ones. The evolutionary account of man's origin seemed to be in direct conflict with certain Christian doctrines. According to Darwin, man has risen from lower forms of life; according to theology, man is a fallen creature, a ruin of something which once was perfect. According to Darwin, man is one among the animals; according to theology, man is unique, fundamentally different from animals in possessing a soul. Even if we believe, as most Christians now do, that the stories of Adam and Eve are profound myths and not literal history, some difficulties remain. The doctrines of the Fall and of the uniqueness of man are not just forced upon Christians because they happen to be there in Genesis 1–3. They are essential pieces of Christian theology, interlocking with a complex integrated system, and cannot be removed without putting the whole structure in jeopardy. It seems, at first sight, as if theology must here come into a head-on collision with the findings of science.

I believe, however, that a better description of what has happened is that theology has here learnt from science, and learnt to its great profit. To admit this is not to sell the theological pass to the scientists, or to allow that in theological matters science must always have the last word. It is simply to recognise that one of the important ways in which God leads us to the truth is through science; and although theologians claim to be able to say some true and valuable things about God and man, they cannot and should not claim to be able to say everything. There are times when they must discover the meaning of their own doctrines with the help of others.

The doctrines of the Fall and of the uniqueness of man *look* as if they were statements about the origins and early history of man, as if they were saying that at some time in the dim, distant past God created a special kind of creature, new things called souls began to exist, and at some point in time the first of these went wrong. It is by no means certain that in the beginnings of Christian theology these doctrines were bound up with these particular historical claims. But by the nineteenth century, and for centuries before that, an overwhelming majority of theologians thought they were. What science did was to help them to think again.

This rethinking has led many modern theologians to see that these doctrines are not speculative pieces of history at all, but statements about the nature of man as he is now. Man is unique because he alone of all creatures desires to enter into relationship with God. The story of how he came to be unique is for science to trace, so far as it can; to understand the story cannot diminish the importance of the fact. Man is fallen, theologians say, because although he desires to enter into relationship with God, he cannot do it. He is divided against himself. The psychological roots of this division are for science to trace, so far as it can; but again, to expose them cannot diminish the importance of fact. Theology is telling us about these present facts of experience from its own distinctive point of view, because it claims to have a decisive clue to the understanding of man, given to it in the unique man, Jesus Christ. That a scientific understanding of the same facts may also be possible, simply illustrates the truth that there are many different ways of understanding things, and that in this field, just as much as in the fields of atomic physics or astronomy, we have to look suspiciously at the assumption that only science can tell us about "reality".

Enough has been said, I hope, to show that the theory of evolution has made a profound difference to theology, as great as that made by Newton's theory of gravitation two hundred years earlier. But it would be a mistake to interpret the religious implications of either of these discoveries just in terms of scientific advance and theological retreat. In both periods theologians had good cause for anxiety; but anxiety is not the same as defeat in battle. The theologians who tried to come to terms with these discoveries made many mistakes, and probably still do. They grasped, however, the important truth that theological doctrines are not, any more than scientific theories are, definitive blueprints of reality. Theology must learn from science, as well as from its own sources, and it is no dishonour or disaster when in the light of science old doctrines are understood in new ways.

Chapter 9

SCIENCE AND THE BIBLE

No sooner was the controversy over Darwinism beginning to warm up than the supporters of ecclesiastical orthodoxy in Britain had to face a new attack, this time from a group of prominent churchmen themselves. *Essays and Reviews*, published in 1860, was a series of essays pleading for a more liberal approach to theology within the Church of England; the essayists stressed that theology was a developing subject which should take account of advances in knowledge, and in particular should welcome the new understanding of the Bible made possible by the work of continental scholars. Today most of the views expressed in the book appear commonplace; but a hundred years ago it was felt to contain ideas which struck at the very root of Christianity. One phrase especially, in the essay by Benjamin Jowett, the Master of Balliol, caused great offence and consternation. He urged that scholars should study and interpret the Bible "like any other book". It is the implications of that phrase which I want to consider in this chapter.

If the Bible *were* just "like any other book", and had no more value than any other book, Christianity would be without foundation. But this is not what Jowett meant, though it is what his opponents tried to twist his words into meaning. His aim was to take it off its pedestal where it had stood for centuries as a book beyond criticism, a source of timeless truths about God. It may be, and Jowett thought it was, a unique source of understanding about God. But it is also a *book*, and as such it should be open to the ordinary methods of literary criticism. To study it like any other book meant to ask questions about how, why and by whom it was written; to compare it with other documents of the period, and the sacred literature of other religions; to try to estimate its historical accuracy and to rediscover the actual religious experiences out of which the writings grew. What Jowett wished to deny was the notion of some special privilege attached to the Biblical writings, which made it impious to take them at anything but their face value.

In all this he, and many of the continental scholars from

whom he drew his inspiration, were in line with the scientific approach to knowledge, with its suspicion of "authorities" and privileged sources of information and claims to uniqueness. Indeed it is possible to read the story of Biblical criticism as the attempt to apply the scientific method to a vital part of Christianity itself, and that is why I believe something about it ought to be included in a book about science and religion. Biblical criticism is not a part of science in the ordinary sense of the word because it deals with a very different kind of subject matter; but there is a way of studying the Bible which tries to make an impartial assessment of the facts, which contrasts and compares as many documents as possible, and which makes use of related scientific subjects like archaeology. This kind of criticism is in a broad sense scientific, more because it captures the mood of science than because of any techniques which it employs. There is a far larger element of personal judgment in it than in, say, physics, and it is far more difficult for critics to reach agreement. But it is not just inspired guesswork, and in the course of time conclusions emerge from it, which win very wide acceptance. Sometimes absurd claims have been made for so-called "scientific criticism", and the assured results of a century ago look distinctly less assured today. But the same could be said of many other sciences, and there seems no good reason to doubt that ancient documents like the Bible can be and have been studied with the same scientific rigour as the more tractable material handled by physics and chemistry.

Such, at any rate, was the belief of those who set out in the nineteenth century to study the Bible as one ancient document among many, and to explain how it came to be. The beginnings of Biblical criticism go back to the middle of the eighteenth century, and many of the difficulties, inconsistencies and contradictions in the Bible, which criticism usually takes as its starting point, were noted even earlier than that. But the results of such study only began to be felt in Britain towards the end of the nineteenth century, and many of them have not penetrated the consciousness of the ordinary Christian even yet. Hence the storm when in 1860 Jowett threatened that reverent and uncritical attitude towards the Book, which till then had seemed the only proper expression of Christian piety.

Perhaps the biggest achievement of the critical movement has been to enable scholars to see the Bible in historical perspective.

Because it comes to us as one book, bound within one set of covers, speaking in roughly the same language throughout, and dignified with titles like "The Word of God", Christians have tended to read it as if it was all addressed to them, and should all be equally relevant. The idea that documents belong to their own times, and should be understood in the light of those times, is a comparatively new one. Applied to the Bible, it means, for example, that we can recognise Abraham's and Isaiah's conceptions of God as different, but related to one another, and different also from the conception which the New Testament gives us. We can come to see the Bible as a body of literature which grew up in the course of a nation's religious development, and which enables us to discover what that religion was all about as we put ourselves in the position of its authors and its original readers. What such an approach destroys is the notion of the Bible as a sort of inspired encyclopaedia, any word of which can be taken out of its context and applied directly to ourselves. Much preaching, unfortunately, encourages this attitude by suggesting that the Bible consists of a series of isolated "texts", which can be made the subjects of a sermon without enquiring when and why they were written.

Until it was possible to study the Bible with this sense of historical perspective, critics found themselves in an uncomfortable dilemma. The objections against accepting the whole book as speaking authoritatively about God in all its parts were becoming more and more pressing. Yet to reject any of it seemed tantamount to suggesting that the Bible contained no more than a collection of religious ideas which could be accepted or rejected at will. Had it in fact any greater value than the Babylonian myths or the chronicles of the Assyrian kings or the sacred books of the East? In the nineteenth century these were flooding into Europe and were beginning to change people's feelings towards ancient documents claiming special authority. If once criticism of the Bible began, where would it stop? Historical understanding did not answer all these questions, but it provided a way of discriminating between different parts of the Bible, and thus seeing what, if anything, in it is unique. And so the way was open for a scientific study of the Bible which did not automatically destroy the basis of faith.

Unfortunately, however, the word "scientific" in this context is ambiguous. I have already suggested a broad sense in which the critical study of any literature can be called scientific. But "the scientific study of the Bible" can also mean the attempt to bring everything recorded in the Bible within the bounds of natural science. And this is a very different thing.

Anthropologists, for example, study primitive religions, and have theories about the evolution of religion from crude beginnings in totemism and animism, through polytheism, up to the so-called higher monotheistic religions. There was a time when it was felt that the Bible ought to conform to this pattern, so the books were searched for traces of animistic belief, the names of the patriarchs were given totemistic significance, anything suggesting monotheism was automatically labelled "late", and the various documents were arranged in chronological order according to the stage of religious development they were thought to reveal. This would have been an admirable theory if it had fitted the facts. But though in one sense it seems scientifically reasonable, and was for a time illuminating, it does not give a satisfactory account of the records as we actually find them in the Bible. Biblical scholars have found increasingly that as a working hypothesis it is a hindrance rather than a help to understanding. I want to emphasize the point that their rejection of it is just as "scientific" as the anthropological theory itself. People who have never studied the Bible seriously sometimes write and speak as if any theory about religion is good enough to "explain" the Bible, provided it looks at least superficially plausible. One hears the wildest guesses put forward as explanations for the origin of the New Testament. Whereas in a "scientific" account, the details of what is actually written ought to receive exhaustive treatment, because these are just as much facts as the facts on which any theory in the natural sciences is based.

In saying this I do not mean to suggest that all or any of the statements in the Bible must be accepted as true. We can be as sceptical about them as we like. But what we must also do is to recognise that they are there, and that they demand an adequate explanation. A great deal of the Old Testament, for example, revolves around the belief that, at a certain point in her history, Israel was delivered from slavery in Egypt when such deliverance seemed highly unlikely. This is ascribed to the work of God, and the motive force which drove the people out on an impossible adventure is said to be faith in God. This is simply a fact about the Old Testament. What the responsible scholar has to do is to weigh up in his own mind, on the one hand the unlikelihood of the events as actually recorded in the Old Testament, and on the other hand the need to find some explanation for the faith which was undoubtedly there. If he is too sceptical about the events, he leaves himself with an impossible job in explaining what is written. Extreme scepticism appears at first sight to be a brave and honest attitude, but extreme sceptics ought to recognise that their approach creates new problems in the act of dismissing old ones.

The same need to find a balance between scepticism and the facts to be explained becomes even more pressing when we turn to the New Testament. Nobody who is genuinely concerned about religious truth can ignore Jesus; it is simply a fact that the writers of the New Testament believed certain remarkable things about Him, that the existence of the Church depends on those beliefs, and that the history of the world has been profoundly influenced by them (to put it at its lowest). Anyone trying to give an adequate account of Jesus must take all this into consideration. Christian theology begins at the point where a thinker recognises that there is a mystery about His person which cannot be explained away without flying in the face of these facts. Christian theologians, on the whole, are not more credulous or less honest than other men, nor do most of them merely search around for any old argument to bolster up beliefs which they already hold. Anybody who takes the trouble to read some of the first-rate critical work done recently on the New Testament will probably be surprised at the distance to which scepticism can go in theological writing. Where a Christian is likely to differ from a non-Christian in his study of the Bible is not in the depth of his scepticism or in the integrity of his scholarship, but in the fact that he knows from the inside something of what the Biblical writers are trying to convey; and this makes him much less ready to dismiss difficult ideas or unlikely claims out of hand. He is a person who feels himself driven to do theology because there are facts which he cannot escape. That other people do find themselves able to escape these facts proves to him that a certain sympathy or inner understanding is needed before their full force can be felt. But, granted that sympathy, the pressure of the facts upon him and the honesty of his response to them, seem no different from, say, the pressure of physical facts upon a physicist.

Perhaps I can illustrate this with a word about miracles. At a certain stage in the history of New Testament criticism it was assumed, for philosophical and scientific reasons, that all accounts of miracles in ancient documents must be false. Miracles were felt to be so offensive to the scientific outlook that it seemed best to explain away all mention of them as caused by ignorance, credulity, misunderstanding or plain mystery-making. It was well known how stories of marvels collect around the names of great men, and it was felt that the miracles of Jesus fell into the same category. New Testament critics, therefore, who started from this assumption, found themselves forced to cut away great sections of the narrative in trying to recover the original simple message of Jesus as it was before pious embroiderers got to work on it. But what they were left with was a picture even more incredible than the miracles which they originally found so unacceptable.

When one actually studies the miracle stories in the New Testament, as opposed to rejecting them on principle, one finds them so closely woven into the story of Jesus, that it is impossible to say this or that was added afterwards as men tried to make His life appear more marvellous. In fact most of such stories in the New Testament are quite different in outlook and purpose from known examples of mystery-making. It has been discovered that the Gospels are not artless tales, mere collections of stories thrown together with a few especially startling ones for good measure. They are very carefully constructed theological works, in which the miracles have a vital place as signs or pointers to the meaning of the coming of Christ. This is why when John the Baptist sent to ask Jesus if he was "the one who should come", the only answer he was given was "the blind receive their sight, the lame walk, the lepers are cleansed. . . ". The Gospel writers hint that there is a very close connection between the miracles which Jesus performed, and the meaning of his mission (see Mark 2: 17). And in St. John's Gospel the connection is made completely clear by calling them "signs" and by surrounding each of them with a long discourse. Thus the feeding of the five thousand, which in St. Mark's Gospel is simply referred to as possessing some mysterious meaning understood only by the disciples (see Mark 8: 19–21), in St.

John is followed by a whole chapter on "The Bread of life" (John 6).

All this is not to prove that the miracles actually happened. But it does show that the Gospel writers were not interested in these stories as mere records of marvels. For them they were an essential part of the Gospel itself, the good news that God was active in Jesus Christ. When a person believes that such activity of God towards His world is not impossible, to reject the New Testament miracles on the grounds that science is suspicious of them seems arbitrary, and in the wider sense of the word, unscientific. It is not being true to the evidence to lump these stories together with all other stories of strange happenings in the lives of popular heroes, and then to dismiss the lot as incredible. It may be that Jesus did all sorts of things, like healing nervous diseases by suggestion, which would not to us nowadays seem so very startling; it may be also that some incidents, like the walking on the water, were misinterpreted or misunderstood or enlarged upon by the early Church. But what seems very difficult to doubt is that the first Christians believed, for what to them seemed good reasons, that the working of God shone through the life of Jesus with special brilliance—and therefore He was able to do strange and marvellous things. And this was summed up for them in their belief that He had risen from the dead.

So far in this chapter I have been trying to draw a distinction between two senses of the word "scientific" as applied to the study of the Bible. I have accepted the broad meaning of the word, the meaning which I believe Jowett intended when he wrote that the Bible should be studied "like any other book". I wish to reject the other, narrower meaning, namely the assumption that everything recorded in the Bible can be explained within the bounds of natural science. I do not believe it is possible to prove conclusively the rightness or wrongness of this assumption; people react to it in ways which depend on their sympathy with or inner understanding of religious experience. To those who find the Christian faith full of meaning for their own lives, the assumption that the laws of natural science must always have the last word, appears intolerably arbitrary. They are prepared to believe that there are mysteries, and especially about the person of Jesus, which science cannot fathom.

But they only know about such mysteries by faith. Faith is

one of those words which cannot be avoided in any discussion of religion. So when I wrote about the results of New Testament criticism, I deliberately wrote, not about this or that having actually happened, but about what the New Testament writers themselves believed to have happened. This is not a weakness, as if one were to say that the evidence on which religion is based is so dubious that faith has to be dragged in as an inferior substitute for scientific knowledge. The Bible itself is a confession of faith. It is the literature of a community which was bound together by its faith in God, which set out to interpret what happened to it in the light of that faith, and which found again and again that its faith was vindicated.

The Bible tells us what happens when we take the life of faith seriously. In many ways it is a very human piece of work, full of the prejudices, exaggerations and misjudgments which belong to every human work. But that is by no means the whole story. One of the most remarkable features of the Bible is that the more one recognises how the people who wrote it were ordinary human beings, the more one becomes aware of the extraordinary insights and experiences with which they were trying to grapple. But there is no way really to discover what those insights were, without to some extent sharing the life and faith of the community whose literature it is.

This is why it is always possible to look at the Bible from some vantage point well outside the life of the Christian community, and to dismiss it as valueless. This is why, also, those who try to defend the Bible against attack often appear prejudiced, and at times have defended it very unwisely. But it is doubtful whether we ever really understand anything without some sort of sympathy for it; and, as I shall argue in a later chapter, even our scientific knowledge presupposes that we share the life and faith of a scientific community, whose deepest insights can only be understood by those who are in it.

Chapter 10

THE LIMITS OF DOUBT

There are people who, when the first glimmerings of scientific understanding begin to dawn in them, immediately have a great feeling of elation and power, and go around smashing religious beliefs with as much gusto as a Cromwellian soldier smashing statues of the Virgin Mary. In the last chapter we saw how people with a complete lack of sympathy for Biblical religion found no difficulty in dismissing it as unworthy of serious attention. Adolescents often go through a similar phase of insensitivity to religion. But all these are relatively crude attitudes. They have their counterpart in the general history of the relation between science and religion in the eighteenth and early nineteenth centuries, when the arguments brought against the Christian faith were mostly of the type—the Bible is not historically or literally true—it is full of inconsistencies—miracles cannot happen—the universe is a great machine—and so forth. These are the arguments which so far have mostly concerned us.

But there are other objections, posed more by the scientific attitude than by particular scientific discoveries, which strike far deeper. There is a kind of scepticism which is profoundly religious in outlook and which, so far from dismissing Christianity as valueless or nonsensical, values it and explains it. "Of course Christians believe so and so," such a sceptic might say, "on their own premises they are quite right; but I will undertake to show why they believe it. I will explain it in psychological or sociological terms, and show how necessary it is for them, and why they need to think it is true, even though it isn't."

In this chapter we shall consider two non-Christian philosophers who explored the limits of doubt by arguing along these lines. The first of them wrote extensively and sympathetically about the Christian faith, and aimed to show its importance while denying that it was anything more than a human invention. The second was obsessed by religion and attacked Christianity with extreme virulence, trying to set up a sort of anti-Christianity of his own. Both of them were nineteenth century Germans, and although it is fashionable to imagine that anything done in the nineteenth century can be done even better in the twentieth, these two remain the classic examples of two kinds of religious doubt.

Feuerbach (1804–1872) has been called "the classical sceptic in theology", and it is he who still haunts modern theology and lurks underneath much modern unbelief. His aim was so to translate theology as to show that God was simply a reflection of man himself. He believed that in doing this he had at last penetrated to the heart of the mystery of religion—"the realization and recognition of theology as anthropology". Religion for him was nothing more than a projection outwards of human hopes and desires and aspirations.

We are all familiar nowadays with this type of explanation of religion as "a projection"; modern accounts of it are usually decked out with a great deal of psychological acumen; but we have Feuerbach to thank for the basic idea. It is important to see that he came to it, not as a cheap argument for dismissing Christianity, but as an insight which for him revealed Christianity's true value. He would have nothing to do with a God who existed over against man. God has no real existence as an object. He is of no value as an explanation of anything in the natural world. The idea of God "explains nothing because it is supposed to explain everything without distinction". God exists only in thought; and when it is seen that all the so-called theological truth about God is really truth about man, then the way is open for a proper valuation of man himself. Instead of being crushed and humiliated by his religion, man ought to be liberated, he ought to be set free to follow his highest ideals, provided always he remembers that these ideals have no existence outside himself. "God is for man the commonplace book where he registers his highest feelings and thoughts, the genealogical album into which he enters the names of the things most dear and sacred to him." God is human nature purified and freed from limitations; He is the gap which man feels when he thinks about his own nature in its finiteness and imperfection.

From here Feuerbach goes on to re-interpret particular Christian doctrines, and each time he leads his readers back to the point where they discover that these doctrines are no more than truths about themselves. The incarnation—this is where theology lets the cat out of the bag, and confesses that God is really man. The mainspring of the incarnation is love, so the doctrine that God sent His son is a roundabout way of saying that the highest value is human love. Grace is "the mystery of chance . . . hence the arbitrariness of grace—the complaint of the pious that grace at one time visits and blesses them, at another for- sakes and rejects them". The Holy Spirit is "the representation of religious emotion, enthusiasm". Prayer is the adoration of man's own heart; it is faith in the absolute reality of our wishes and emotions.

And so on. Throughout Feuerbach's writings the same formula is applied. Theology is stood on its head. Everything is referred back to man.

Feuerbach is thus a key figure in the so-called nineteenth century "religion of humanity". At a time when it was becom- ing increasingly difficult for those influenced by science to be- lieve that God actually did anything in a world governed by iron necessity, religious feeling found an outlet in the redis- covery of the importance of man. There is a religious wistfulness about the agnostic writers of that period; there is a religious concern about human betterment; and where shreds of religious faith remain, morality makes up nine-tenths of it. "Religion is morality touched with emotion" in Matthew Arnold's famous definition. And essentially the same view is held by very large numbers of people today, who have probably never heard of either Feuerbach or Matthew Arnold, but who think that the heart of Christianity is living a decent life, who would say that love is their supreme value, and who have no use for specula- tions about God.

I do not intend to argue very much against Feuerbach because there is a sense in which religion must always be open to his kind of criticism. If religion concerns us deeply as human be- ings, then it must be theoretically possible to give an account of it in terms of human feelings and the fulfilment of human needs. If this were not so, then it would not be *our* religion. Feuerbach wrote at a time when German theology had been concerning itself almost exclusively with the analysis of "the religious consciousness", following the lead given by Schleier- macher (see page 53 seq.), and was thus wide open to his re- interpretation. If Christianity is no more than a product of "the religious consciousness", then Feuerbach is right.

But the community of faith, which was described at the end of the last chapter, was not simply analysing its own feelings and desires as it produced the Bible and lived by faith in God. It was reacting to events which had actually happened to it; and in particular the early Christians were reacting to a man, Jesus, whom their leaders had actually known. It is true that there are difficulties when one tries to say precisely what happened and what did not, because we have no means of knowing the events except through the eyes of believers. But we can be certain that the first believers themselves thought they were responding to facts, and not to inventions of their "religious consciousness". Feuerbach simply highlights the need for Christians to stress the historical basis of their faith.

It is significant too that he has virtually nothing to say about sin and evil, in striking contrast to the Bible. The God of the Bible is no mere projection of human hopes and aspirations. He challenges and disturbs men; He judges them as sinners; He is holy and unapproachable; He is radically unlike man, and can be known only as He reveals Himself in the act of transforming men into what they could never become by themselves. To anybody for whom the essence of Christianity is found in the individual man as a sinner with no claims over God, who is nevertheless grasped by God in an act of sheer undeserved love, Feuerbach's analysis seems to be plainly irrelevant.

Since Feuerbach's day theology has moved more in this direction, no doubt partly in reaction against him. The so-called neo-orthodox movement in theology laid great emphasis on the complete separation between God and man, a gulf which can be bridged only by God Himself. This is a genuine insight which has always been part of Christianity; but the fact that sceptics like Feuerbach had to prod theologians into rediscovering it, illustrates once again the continual interplay between theology and all sorts of other ways of thinking. Theology is not a fixed system of timeless truths. It is the attempt, always inadequate, to express the faith of a community which is rooted in certain historical events, and which shares certain insights and experiences. Those who doubt and criticise and explain away this faith, may win others to their point of view. But they generally also provoke a reaction from those who find the criticisms deepening their insight into what they believe, by showing up the inadequacy of their expression of it. Thus it is a mistake to think of Feuerbach either as a thinker who can be refuted, or as one who finally explains away religion.

He is the representative of a certain kind of doubt which shows up the human elements in religion for what they are.

The other sceptic I want to consider in this chapter took his criticisms of Christianity very much further, even to the extent of attacking Christian values and morality, as well as Christian doctrine. Nietzsche (1844–1900) was an atheist in the most profound sense of the word. He really saw what it meant to live in a world without God; he did not, like so many, merely push his scepticism to the point where it ceased to be convenient. In fact he was even contemptuous of other atheists who had "dropped God like a chance acquaintance". For him the absence of God was the most important fact about the world, and one which haunted him all his life.

With the absence of God went an absence of belief in any ultimate truth. Nietzsche believed that we can have no knowledge of reality because our view of the world is entirely conditioned by our needs and the accidents of our development. Metaphysicians and scientists try to make sense of the world because we all long for stability and order. "The will to truth is merely the longing for a stable world." But there is no reason to suppose that this longing must necessarily be satisfied, or that the world contains any sense for us to discover. It may be, as Nietzsche said it was, that everything is ultimately meaningless; and if this seems intolerable, what right have we to complain? Why should we assume that the world *ought* to be tolerable? To complain presupposes that there is some ultimate order and justice, which is precisely what Nietzsche wished to deny. The only truth or order or values which a man can have are those which he himself creates.

If God is dead (killed by Nietzsche) and truth does not exist, man becomes responsible for all that is. In this sense, we create our own world. Whatever order or meaning we find in it, we ourselves have put there. Man, for Nietzsche, is his own God, the only source of values and morality. "He who no longer finds what is great in God will find it nowhere—he must either deny it or create it." Or as Dostoevsky put it, writing at about the same time, "Where there is no God, all things are lawful."

Even science did not escape his criticism. Scientists imagine, he said, that they are discovering the structure of reality. In fact they are only imposing their own interpretations on the world, finding regularities which exist only in their own minds,

driven on by their own needs. "The object (of science) is not to
know but to schematize—to impose as much regularity and
form upon chaos, as our practical needs require." This becomes
clear as soon as one asks the meaning of the ultimate terms
which science uses. "Force", "attraction", "energy" are all
notions which derive from human experience. Causality is our
device for escaping our fear of the unfamiliar, by relating it to
something which is already known. The mechanistic picture of
the universe is an illusion; the ultimate reality is chaos, and our
scientific theories are no more than instruments which enable
us to manipulate it, and which give us a sense of security.

Not everyone, of course, can rise to the heights of seeing all
this, of admitting that reality is meaningless chaos, and can
nevertheless go on to impose their own meaning upon it and
"create a world". Looking back, Nietzsche saw a handful of
great men who had shaped our interpretation of reality; and for
the future he put his trust in a new kind of man, superman, who
would have the courage to accept his insights and live by them
positively and creatively. Nietzsche would have nothing to do
with the mass of men who meekly accepted any interpretation
provided it was comfortable and kept them happy; and in particularly he violently rejected the Christian values of meekness,
respect for the weak, humility before God—what he called the
Christian "slave morality". The Christian idea of God was intolerable to him, because it seemed to devalue man. "If there
were gods, how could I endure not to be god! Therefore there
are no gods."

Nietzsche takes us to the logical conclusion of atheism. His
superman is really a god-man. He rejects God but he cannot
escape Him. His scepticism takes him right down to the bot-
tom of the abyss, where the only god is himself.

His importance is that he shows us how many of our ordinary
beliefs about the world, our belief in its rationality, our notion
of truth, our system of values, are bound up with belief in God
—and when this goes, everything goes. In this sense, Nietzsche
was a profoundly religious thinker, for whom Christians can be
grateful. By stressing our own rôle in shaping the world as we
know it, he drew attention to a feature of human knowledge
which even science itself has begun to recognise. I believe he
was exaggerating when he stated that our knowledge was *completely* shaped by our own needs and the accidents of our

development; we can admit that we always interpret reality from our special point of view, without agreeing that our interpretations are mere invention. But in spite of his exaggerations he raised problems in the philosophy of science, about the relation between scientific theories and reality, which are still very much live issues.

By his bitter accusation that Christianity devalues man and encourages a slave-like attitude, he put his finger on the weak spot in a certain kind of theology. As we saw when considering Feuerbach, a theology which fails to take seriously man's separation from God and his inability to help himself, is open to re-interpretation as a projection of human wishes. But a theology which concentrates exclusively on human separation and weakness falls into the opposite error, and comes under Nietzsche's axe; it takes the nerve out of human effort; it makes men sceptical about their chances of being able to improve the human lot before they have even begun. A great many people still think this way about Christianity, and reject it because they believe they will be able to do more good in the world by thinking the best of human nature than by thinking the worst.

The New Testament, however, neither thinks the best of human nature, nor the worst—or rather it thinks both. Its tremendous emphasis on man's weakness is balanced by its vision of his limitless possibilities in Christ. It is profoundly pessimistic about human nature as it exists by itself; it is almost unbelievably optimistic about what God can do through human beings transformed by His power. Rather than showing us, as Nietzsche did, a picture of man trying to pretend that he is God, it shows us man becoming what he was meant to be as a child and partner of God, co-operating in God's work of creation.

To make this contrast is not to prove that the New Testament vision of man is correct. But it is worth noting that the practical examples we have seen of Nietzsche's superman have not been very encouraging. Hitler was one of them; and at least some of his monstrosities can be ascribed to his Nietzschean belief that he was above the law. Right and wrong were what Hitler decided they were—and we know what he decided. It seems to be a fact that those who think of themselves as God cease to be tolerable even as men. Whereas those who think of themselves as under God can rise to the heights without losing their humanity.

These remarks, like those about Feuerbach, are not intended to be a refutation of Nietzsche. One cannot refute somebody who resolutely pushes religious scepticism to its extreme limit. One can only watch him coming full circle, and becoming more and more obsessed by the God whom he thinks he has rejected. This is one of the great arguments for the truth of religion. It is only a very shallow kind of scepticism, a deliberate concentration on the surface appearance of things, which can feel satisfied when it has dismissed the whole religious side of life as worthless. Scientists, particularly young ones who are in the first flush of excitement about their discoveries, are especially liable to make this sort of mistake. Practical questions about the precise relationship between one thing and another seem so much more manageable and profitable, that the more searching philosophical and religious questions look as if they can safely be dismissed. But nobody can really be concerned about the truth without being concerned about it *religiously*, as Nietzsche himself demonstrates. This is why sceptics of his calibre show up the superficiality of much modern religious doubt in a far more telling manner than could be done by any amount of religious exhortation.

Chapter 11

THE RISE OF TECHNOLOGY

"The greatest invention of the nineteenth century was the invention of the method of invention." Professor Whitehead there put his finger on the essential difference between modern technology and all the technical achievements of previous ages. Men have always made use of technology. According to anthropologists, man is a tool-making animal; his technological skill is what makes him man. There have been times in human history when this skill has reached very high levels; in fact all the really brilliant and fundamental technological discoveries were made long before the nineteenth century. The making of fire, the wheel, the lever, the uses of wind and water, methods of building and time-keeping, all these go back to the earliest days of civilisation. Ancient Chinese civilisation was familiar with a host of inventions: magnetism was known and used by the second century A.D. and examples of printing survive from the ninth century. Technology, therefore, certainly was not invented in Victorian England. The revolution, which Whitehead drew attention to, lay in the systematic application of scientific principles to technological problems.

The emphasis is on the word "systematic". Up till then discovery and invention had been relatively haphazard affairs. Individual men of genius, like Watt with his steam engine, had seen new possibilities in familiar things. The various arts and crafts and trades, like the building trade, had evolved slowly throughout the centuries, and had gradually improved their techniques. But the immense burst of technological progress, which has transformed the world in a hundred years, was only possible when scientific discoveries began to be applied to practical problems in scientific ways.

Men have always used drugs, for example. Up till fairly recently the vast majority of drugs were naturally-occurring substances whose properties had become known by chance. By contrast, the modern drug industry is almost wholly a branch of applied chemistry, in which tens of thousands of chemical formulae are systematically varied and tested in order to pro-

duce the right combination of properties. The original discovery which starts a new line of research may still be acciden-
tal, as happened with penicillin; but this discovery sparked off
a systematic research programme which produced all the varie-
ties of antibiotics in use today.

The systematic approach to technological problems has not
cut out the rôle of the individual inventor or discoverer; but it
has enormously accelerated the rate of progress. And it has
completely changed the social status of science and scientists.

Nobody can ignore science nowadays, because we are all surrounded by the fruits of it, and we recognise it as one of the most
powerful forces in the modern world. Scientists are no longer
regarded as rather odd amateurs who dabble about in laboratories. With the rise of technology has come scientific profes-
sionalism and specialisation. The commercial value of science,
and the fact that there is plenty of scientific work which can be
done by people of very ordinary intelligence, has led to a vast in-
crease in the number of scientists; and these are now accepted as
an essential part of a healthy society. Even as recently as thirty
years ago, there were schools where the science department was
regarded as the abode of a few strange people who had unfortunately been allowed to escape from the full rigours of a
classical education. Today, it is classics which is fighting for its
life. Science not only seems to attract the best brains in the
country, but also seems to hold out the best prospects of future
employment. And we are continually being reminded how the
power and influence of the various nations in the world of the
future will depend more and more on the extent and quality of
their science.

All this has considerable religious implications. In the early
days of science, discoveries and speculations about the nature
of the world were of interest to an educated minority. Some
scientific ideas filtered down to the level of ordinary people;
but it was always possible to ignore them, or at least to mini-
mise their effect. Most people's feelings about the world continued much as they were before, or changed so gradually that
there was no sharp sense of conflict. Today, on the other hand,
science is part of our everyday lives; its successes are obvious
for everyone to see. Even people who have had no formal
scientific education cannot fail to be impressed. As practical
ways of getting things done, science and religion do not seem

to bear comparison. In a country suffering from drought, a thousand years of prayer for rain are less effective than one well thought-out irrigation scheme.

That last contrast may seem to be rather cheap. Prayer ought not to mean that we stop using our brains or trying to help ourselves. But there is no doubt that popular religion looks for prayer to work miracles; and when it sees science working miracles instead, science becomes its god. There is a sad story about a Chinaman who for years had prayed for prosperity to a metal image, with noticeably little success. After the Communist revolution he sent his god to the local engineering works, hoping that in the form of ball-bearings it would be rather more use. That is a parable of what many people have done with far more sophisticated notions of God. Technology has brought the scientific revolution home to us. We have learnt to judge things in terms of their practical usefulness. This is perhaps why so much modern criticism of Christianity dismisses it with the words "ineffective" and "irrelevant", and does not concern itself in any depth with the truth or otherwise of its claims.

With this shift of emphasis from the theoretical to the practical, goes a change in the character of science itself. Science has always had two aims—knowledge and power; and these are closely connected. Knowledge brings power, and power implies knowledge. To understand the mechanism of heredity, for example, opens up possibilities of controlling it, and producing genetic changes at will. In the same way, to be able to release nuclear energy shows that, in spite of all the uncertainties about the nature of ultimate particles, our concept of the atomic nucleus corresponds in some sense with physical reality. To this extent, knowledge and power go hand in hand, and are not two entirely different things. But the precise relationship between them is not at all clear.

We have already seen how the early scientists assumed that they were discovering the nature of reality. The fact that their theories led to practical results was for them the proof that this was the way things really were. Many modern scientists take exactly the opposite view; they are not nearly so sure that they can say anything about reality at all. They regard their theories as useful guides, as tools which enable them to manipulate nature, whether they are true in any ultimate sense or not. According to such a view, truth is "what works". An idea is to be judged by its practical value. So-called pure science builds a vast theoretical structure which finds its ultimate vindication in technology. Knowledge is a step on the road to power, rather than power a by-product and test of knowledge.

To some extent this contrast is embodied in the contrast between academic and applied scientists. The contrast can be overdone; but there is an important difference between the man who feels himself free to do fundamental research, to find out things for the sake of finding them out, and the man who is looking for the solution to a particular practical problem. Academic scientists, who may spend years studying some minute and apparently remote corner of nature, usually justify themselves in public by saying that no one can tell what useful applications any piece of research might eventually have; but what actually keeps them going is curiosity and a belief, however muddled, that in some sense they are discovering the truth, and that this is worthwhile as an end in itself.

Scientists and philosophers of science are still very much divided among themselves over the precise relationship between the two aims of science, and theologians would be very foolish if they took sides. But it is worth stressing again the complexity of the relation between science and theology, by noting a few of the theological consequences of different scientific attitudes. When the emphasis is on science as a search for truth, theologians can point out that this is itself a sort of religious activity. Science and theology unite in taking seriously questions about the nature of reality and in believing that answers of some sort are possible. They only fall out with each other when one or both of them claims that its kind of truth is the only "real truth" or the only truth worth having. Because this was the claim which some scientists and philosophers were making explicitly by the end of the nineteenth century, theologians welcomed with relief the changed view of science, which saw it as a quest for power, not concerned with ultimate realities at all. This seemed to leave the field free for theology. There are many books in defence of the Christian faith, which first make great play with the limitations of scientific knowledge, and then call in theology to provide answers where science cannot. But such an approach reckons without the fact that agnosticism in science often breeds agnosticism in religion as well.

It is no coincidence, I believe, that agnosticism, as a widespread attitude, was born in the mid-nineteenth century, at the very time of greatest technical acceleration. The new-found sense of power made men impatient with the old arguments about the nature of reality. It was possible to ignore these, and get on with the job of improving the world and making practical decisions; it was even possible to talk about progress without being sure precisely what was progressing in what direction. Marx put into words the assumption which unconsciously controlled many people's attitude: "The philosophers have only *interpreted* the world, in various ways; the point, however, is to *change* it." It seemed that religious and philosophical subtleties could be safely by-passed, because they were no longer relevant to practical life.

Now, in the mid-twentieth century, it is difficult to be so certain that this is true. Our age has become more and more conscious of the ambiguity of human power. We have had several startling examples of the difficulties of controlling power, and of the dangers of thinking we know more than we do. I do not need to labour the problems which nuclear energy poses for us. A more recent example is our present concern about the pollution of the environment. Again, it is feared that the prolonged use of some insecticides may lead to the evolution of resistant strains of insects, and the elimination of many species of animals, including those which normally keep the insect population in check. The last state may therefore be far worse than the first. A very different kind of example is the power of selective breeding which some eugenicists would like to apply to human beings.

In all these examples there are both practical and moral problems intertwined. A convinced pest-control enthusiast, for instance, might say that with the progress of science it will be possible to outwit the insects in the next round of the fight against them, even more successfully than DDT was able to do it in the first round. But this is to overlook the moral and practical issues, whether it is wise to work with nature or against it, whether it is right to exterminate large numbers of other animals, or even species, by using such blunt instruments in the fight against certain pests. The moral issue cannot be decided by science alone. The way we treat it depends on our beliefs about man's place in nature, and ultimately brings us back to those religious and philosophical subtleties which practical science ignores.

Similarly, the problems of selective human breeding are not merely practical. The main obstacle to be overcome is not, as Sir Julian Huxley has rather naïvely suggested, the vanity and prejudice of the husband who would like to be the father of his wife's children. The whole subject bristles with quite fundamental questions about what we believe human beings are, and what value we put on the relationships between them.

Apart from such special, and somewhat lurid, problems there is also nowadays an increasing general uneasiness about the way in which technological advance sets the pace of modern life. Most of us, whether we like it or not, are forced into certain behaviour patterns because these are what our machines demand of us. Some machines can only operate efficiently if they are run continuously; hence shift-work in factories; hence, also, the artificial stimulation of consumption to ensure that the machine is kept busy. Motor cars, radios, telephones and all the rest of the familiar modern devices have completely changed millions of people's lives, and it would be ridiculous to deny that on the whole they have vastly improved human life and increased human possibilities. But it is also worth asking occasionally who is really the master, man or his inventions? And, faced with so many possibilities, what are the essential human values which ought to guide our choice?

While technology once helped to breed an atmosphere of agnosticism, therefore, it also raises in especially urgent forms some of the questions which religion has traditionally tried to answer. Some years ago I had a striking illustration of this when I asked the members of a school science society to send me a series of questions on science and religion. There were some of the old favourites, mostly based on rather naïve interpretations of the Bible, but over half the questions were about the moral choices confronting scientists in the practical uses of their discoveries. It seemed to me then that the wheel had gone full circle, and that what really concerned these boys was the Christian criticism of science, rather than vice versa. Perhaps they were untypical. But, as I have said many times already in this book, religious and philosophical questions have a way of refusing to be ignored. And this is why men go on wrestling with them in spite of all their difficulty, and in spite of the superficial attractions of the practical scientific approach.

Chapter 12

MINDS AND MACHINES

"I want you to meet Horace," said the engineer, "there is virtually no difference between him and a human being."

I looked at Horace, a formidable array of panels and switches stretching the whole length of the room. Outwardly it was only too obvious that Horace was not a human being and, however complex the maze of wires and cells behind those panels, I could not believe that it could even begin to behave like one. I knew, of course, that Horace could play chess or compose a tune; computers had been able to do that sort of thing even back in the early 1960s. But there are many types of human behaviour which we label "mechanical" anyway, and I remember how early machine-made music had been dismissed with just that adjective; it was hack stuff, hardly worthy to be called music at all. I put some of my doubts into words.

"Horace can do much better than that", came the reply. "Modern computers go through a long process of programming. We feed them on the best music and literature, in much the same way as you educate a child. And then with their built-in randomisers we find them throwing up genuinely new ideas, which their programming enables them to recognise and select. I doubt whether a critic nowadays could tell the difference between the music Horace produces and the stuff churned out by living composers."

"Very interesting," I said. "You mean to say that Horace can make real decisions about what is good or bad musically?"

"No difficulty about that," said the engineer. "It's all a question of learning from experience, and a machine can do that as well as a human—in fact better, because it has a far more reliable memory."

"But surely it doesn't understand what it's doing?"

"It depends on what you mean by understanding. If you mean the ability to relate the things you have learnt to other things, then Horace can do that as well as you can."

I was getting desperate by this time, and I gave one of the panels in front of me a kick. "Well, anyway it's got no feelings."

"Not that sort of feeling, certainly," went on the engineer in his maddeningly superior way, "but the funny thing is that the other day we asked him to make a very difficult decision, and lots of contradictory answers came out, almost as if he was agitated and couldn't make up his mind. Whereas other sorts of work he just laps up."

A little green light gleamed balefully, and I was almost certain Horace winked. I began to wish it would lap up the engineer. He was still talking.

"Horace has quite a personality, you know. The other day he said to me 'Anything you can do, I can do better', but that was only pride." The green light glowed even brighter, and for the first time the engineer noticed it. "I am sorry, sir," he added quickly to Horace, "I was only joking."

And then I realised for the first time who was master.

.   .   .   .   .

Was that a fantasy, or a real glimpse of the future? There seems little doubt that in principle Horace's claim "anything you can do I can do better" has a good deal of truth in it. Already computers are able to make calculations and predictions which are far too difficult or laborious for human mathematicians. Machines which could mimic the whole vast range of human activity would have to be so inconceivably complex and costly that they may never be built; but many engineers believe that in principle there is no reason why they should not. They believe that the human brain works in essentially the same way as a computer; and therefore it can have no fundamental properties which cannot be reduced to the terms of electrical engineering.

For some Christians these claims have seemed as alarming as the claims made about the physico-chemical basis of life. But I believe their fears are unnecessary. Just as the living cell is undoubtedly a highly complex chemical system in which it is foolish to look for some extra "vital principle", so the human brain seems to behave very much like a highly complex computer; and as long as we are considering its performance as an analyser, calculator, predictor or decision maker, there is no need to look any further for some extra "mental factor". In the study of brain function the most useful terms, at the moment, are those drawn from this particular branch of engineering.

But the study of brain function is not the same as the study

of the mind, just as the study of life processes is not the same as
the experience of being alive. The words "brain" and "mind"
are not simply interchangeable, though I know one physiologist
who thought he was making a useful contribution to knowledge
by using the word "brain" where anyone else would have used
"mind"; in fact he was simply spreading confusion. No doubt,
what is going on in our brain is directly related to what is going
on in our mind, and vice versa; but we know about them in
quite different ways, one from the outside and the other from
the inside. Both types of knowing give us a partial picture of the
whole, but they must not be confused. We talk about "thought"
and "consciousness" because we think and are conscious; the
words describe part of our direct experience. We talk about
"electrical changes in nervous tissue" because we have learnt to
interpret, say, the patterns on an oscillograph screen, in a certain
way; the words are part of our interpreted sense experience. We
must not simply transfer words used to describe one kind of
experience to contexts where we are discussing the other kind,
without being very careful about what we are doing; otherwise
we might find ourselves talking about monstrosities like
"thoughts three feet square" or "cheerful electrons".

The confusions which people actually fall into, of course, are
much more subtle than these. Some words are particularly
tempting because they are so easy to transfer; for example,
words like "predict" and "analyse". We know what it is to
predict, by predicting. We can also arrive at a fairly objective
definition of prediction, say, in mechanical terms; and for most
purposes we can ignore the different origins of the two uses.

Now along comes an electrical engineer who builds a predicting machine and compares its performance with ours. We admit
that it predicts. And similarly with analysis, calculation, decision making, etc. The engineer then builds a machine which can
do all these things, and plays his trump card. "What is thinking
but a combination of prediction, analysis, calculation, decision
making, etc.? Aren't you forced to admit that my machine can
think?"

Our instinctive reaction is probably to feel that the question
is absurd, and I believe that that reaction is right. But many
people fail to see how the trick has been played. By breaking
down the notion of "thought" into a large number of com-
ponents, and each time glossing over the difference between, say,

prediction as experienced and prediction as described in a machine, it is eventually possible to arrive at a description of "thinking" which leaves out the subjective element altogether. We *seem* to be asking a queer question about the inner life of a computer, whereas the engineer is in fact answering a different question about the number of different kinds of operation which the computer can perform.

Yet it is not simply a confusion of terms which underlies questions like "Do machines think?" or "Are computers conscious?" Granted that there is a big difference between our inner and outer experience, between what we know as true within ourselves, and what we investigate in the world around us, the fact is that we do not use this language of inner experience only about ourselves. We use it of other people. We say not only "I think" but "John and Mary think". So why shouldn't we say "Horace the computer thinks"?

This brings us to the edge of one of the stickiest problems of philosophy. How do we know that other people think and feel as we do? To avoid turning this chapter into a long philosophical discourse I am simply going to expound what I believe to be the most convincing answer to the problem, without arguing it in any detail. It is a fairly common answer nowadays, so perhaps argument is not necessary anyway.

We know that other people think, partly by deducing it from their behaviour. When we ask an attendant in Madame Tussaud's to show us the exit, and receive only a waxy stare in reply, a very simple deduction shows us our mistake. In much the same way in fairy stories the prince was sometimes able to deduce, by studying behaviour, that a particularly loathsome-looking frog was in fact a princess going through an awkward spell. In both cases behaviour gives the clue to what, if anything, is going on inside.

But this is only part of the answer. In particular cases, when we feel we may have been deceived or mistaken, we go through a process of deduction. This is not what happens, though, in our general relationships with other people. We do not first become aware of our own experience of thinking, and then by observing our behaviour and comparing it with that of others, go on to deduce that they think as we do. I believe it is much nearer the truth to say that our knowledge of ourselves is completely bound up with our knowledge of others. We grow up and become what we are in relationship with other people; without that relationship we should not become human beings at all. When, as has sometimes happened, children have been brought up by wolves, completely cut off from human society, they seem to be lacking in any sort of human self-awareness. It is human society which makes us human; and human society presupposes a recognition of one another as basically alike.

The important word in that last sentence is "presupposes". In talking about our knowledge of other people through our general relationships with them, I am not talking about some mysterious sixth sense which enables us to know what is going on in their minds. I am talking about a *presupposition* of social life, and one that is so basic that without it we could not even have an individual human consciousness in ourselves. In other words, we know that other people in general have minds, as directly and certainly as we know it of ourselves.

But how do we have this relationship with other people? One of its great instruments is language. In particular cases we judge what people are thinking by what they say. And this has led some people to question the claim to direct knowledge of other people's minds by asserting that we do, after all, only know what is going on in them through their behaviour. Isn't talking a sort of behaviour?

True. And it is true also that language is almost our only clue to the *contents* of people's minds. But the point is that it is a kind of behaviour which, if it is to be significant for us, already presupposes that our minds are to some extent alike—that we mean roughly the same things by the same words. Language presupposes society and a realm of shared experience. Insofar as we ourselves do a great deal of our thinking in words, or concepts closely related to language, even our own private thoughts presuppose the society in which our minds have been formed, and carry with them the built-in assumption that other people can share the same kind of experience.

There is a sense, then, in which the question "How do we know that other people think and feel as we do?" is an unreal one. We know it directly, and if we did not know it we should not know that we thought or felt ourselves.

When we ask the same question of Horace, the engineer, as we have seen, is tempted to answer in terms of Horace's behaviour. But this is not the only test. We may admit that

Horace behaves like us in many respects, but deny that we can
enter the same kind of relationship with him that we have with
another human being. "He's very clever," we say disparagingly,
"but he's only a machine. He isn't one of us." In other words,
we don't value him as a human person; we don't recognise a
kinship with him; he doesn't belong to that world of personal
relationships which has made us what we are. Our puzzlement
about him brings out into the open an element in human relationships which so far has not been mentioned—the element of
respect.

We understand a machine best by a rigidly objective analysis
of its mode of operation. We also need to know something about
the intentions of its designer. We cannot say that we fully
understand it until we know what it is meant to do. Such respect
as we have for a machine is generally respect for the skill and
ingenuity of the men who designed and constructed it.

We come to understand human beings in many different ways
and on many different levels. For some purposes it is quite
sufficient merely to analyse their mode of operation. But there
are certain levels of understanding which are only possible to
those who are prepared to approach other people with respect
and sympathy, even with a touch of awe. There is a knowledge
which comes, not by rigidly objective analysis, but by opening up
to another person and allowing oneself to be changed. This is
not scientific knowledge. But it is just as real and fundamental
a part of our experience as the more humdrum data which are
the ordinary stuff of scientific analysis.

Why do we respect human beings, and learn things through
our respect, while we refuse the same kind of respect to machines?
I believe the answer is ultimately religious. For Christians every
human being is "made in the image of God" and is a person
"for whom Christ died". Therefore Christians are committed
to a way of life which emphasises as much as possible the unique
value of each individual. There is no way of proving that everyone is worthy of respect, except by seeing how this attitude fits
into a general religious outlook. Similarly there may be no way
of proving that certain computers ought not to be called human,
and vice versa, except by seeing that human beings, whether
they work like computers or not, have a unique status given
them by God. To act on this belief, and to treat others with this
kind of godly respect, is, as I have already said, to open up new

depths of personal knowledge which carry their own conviction of truth. But the initial step is an act of religious faith. Note, however, that this is not faith in a mysterious something inside the human brain, which an engineer can never manufacture to put inside one of his machines. It is faith in the rightness of an attitude to adopt towards human beings, based on the belief that God values those human beings in a certain way. We may respect the performance of computers, and value them very highly indeed in terms of cash, but unless I am very much mistaken most people would regard godly respect as dangerous idolatry.

I have said nothing in this chapter about Christian belief in the soul. A discussion on the level of "Do computers and/or human beings have souls?" would have focused attention on the existence or otherwise of "the mysterious something in the human brain", which is just the sort of thing I have tried to avoid. My aim has been to show how by talking about minds and machines, and by investigating the roots of our uneasiness at extravagant claims made on behalf of the machine, we eventually find ourselves back at religion. But the religious questions which have emerged are genuinely religious ones: "Why do we value human beings?": not quasi-scientific questions about "mysterious somethings". And it is this first kind of question which Christian language about the soul is trying to answer, even though it is often treated as if it were an example of the latter. Belief in the soul, in other words, expresses a Christian's awareness that he can enter into relationship with God, and his intention to treat himself and all men as uniquely valued by God. It is an object of faith, not of scientific knowledge, because it concerns our personal relationships and our intentions; and these are spheres in which faith is not a second-best road to knowledge; it is the only road there is.

If we choose to treat human beings like computers and computers like human beings, it is difficult to think of any watertight arguments which could dissuade us. There is the practical objection that we might find the computers very much more efficient at their jobs than we are at ours—and then the question of who was master might cease to be merely whimsical. But presumably if we really believed that there was no essential difference between men and machines, this is a conclusion we might welcome.

To say that the only defence against this sort of view is to have faith in the value and possibilities of men, is not to be obscurantist or escapist. It is to state the only conditions under which it is possible to get close enough to men for their value and the depths of their personal lives to become apparent. It is to choose *not* to treat human beings like computers, and to discover that experience vindicates the choice.

Chapter 13

AFTER FREUD

"While the different religions wrangle with one another as to which of them is in possession of the truth, in our view the truth of religion may be altogether disregarded. Religion is an attempt to get control over the sensory world, in which we are placed, by means of the wish-world, which we have developed inside us as a result of biological and psychological necessities. But it cannot achieve its end. Its doctrines carry with them the stamp of the times in which they originated, the ignorant childhood days of the human race. Its consolations deserve no trust. Experience teaches us that the world is not a nursery. The ethical commands, to which religion seeks to lend its weight, require some other foundation instead, for human society cannot do without them, and it is dangerous to link up obedience to them with religious beliefs. If one attempts to assign to religion its place in man's evolution, it seems not so much to be a lasting acquisition as a parallel to the neurosis which the civilized individual must pass through on his way from childhood to maturity."

In that paragraph in his *New Introductory Lectures on Psycho-Analysis*, Freud put in a nutshell his estimate of religion. Whereas other sciences, in his opinion, had led to a world view which made the claims of religion incredible, psycho-analysis had administered the *coup de grâce* by showing why, despite the evidence of their senses, men believed it. Religion was a hangover from the helplessness of childhood; it was to be put away with other childish things.

Such an estimate was not new. Freud had plenty of predecessors; among them we have already met Feuerbach, who sought not so much to confront religion with specific objections, as to explain it away by showing its psychological attractiveness. But what made Freud's researches a turning point in the history of thought was his demonstration of the extent to which we are controlled by unconscious and irrational forces. After Freud it is no longer enough merely to avoid being consciously hypocritical; it is no longer enough to be alert to the dangers of believing merely because belief is attractive. Freud revealed a

102

new depth of complexity in the human mind, and of the mind's almost limitless powers of hiding its true motives from itself. And therefore, whether or not he was right in detail, as in many respects he certainly was not, after Freud things can never be quite the same as they were before.

This is an important point to grasp, because Freud has been proved wrong in so many of his judgments, and his theory of religion as a collective neurosis has been criticised so devastatingly, that it is easy for Christians to feel that the challenge of Freudian thought has been met effectively, and no more needs to be done. To believe this is to live in a fool's paradise. Freudianism can no more be met and answered once for all by Christians than Feuerbach can be proved conclusively wrong. Both reveal, in different depths, the way in which the religious mind works; and the insights of both are permanent additions to our understanding. After Freud we know, as was not known before, how deeply religion is coloured by childhood experiences; we have been shown how easily it can become an escape from the world of adult responsibilities. We have learnt to look at morality with new eyes; we see how an excessive uprightness can become a cover for guilt and fear. We have been taught to look beneath the surface of men's acts and words, and find evidence of hidden forces and unacknowledged conflicts. Freud, in other words, opened up an extra dimension in our understanding of human beings, and this is why he deserves to be ranked with Newton and Darwin as an inventor of a new kind of scientific explanation. We grasp his significance for Christianity best, not by confronting Freudian theories with Christian doctrines, but by trying to discover what it means to live and think in the light of this extra dimension.

Suppose, for example, we find someone feeling passionately about a moral issue like society's treatment of homosexuals, and even writing letters to the daily papers denouncing the idea of changing the law, stressing the danger to civilised society, common decency, national security, etc., etc. Before Freud, we should probably have admired him for his high moral sense; nowadays we are more likely to ask what he is hiding. Does he feel strongly about homosexuality because he is genuinely and rationally convinced that it ought to be completely suppressed? Or is he unconsciously afraid and ashamed of homosexual tendencies in himself? And so is he urging his public protestations as a way of saying that his own homosexuality ought to be suppressed?

Is another man's emphasis on the justice of God and the wickedness of sin the fruit of firm conviction about the moral ordering of the universe? Or did he simply have an autocratic father? Or is he tormented by inner feelings of guilt, which make him believe that sin must be punished, because he wants to be punished himself?

This kind of explanation can easily get out of hand, and it is tempting to bandy about words like "rationalisation" and "compensation", which seem to offer a magic formula for disposing of all convictions and questioning all judgments. But to go to such extremes, to deny that there can ever be rational convictions or honest judgments, is to go a very long way beyond the scientific evidence. It is an example of the popularisation and misuse of science, which we met in Chapter 4, when considering the use made of Newton's discoveries. Every science suffers from popular misuse; and psychology more than most.

Nevertheless, despite the dangers of its misuse, the question-mark which psychology puts against the surface appearances of things undoubtedly remains its most serious challenge to religion.

Claims to religious experience are especially vulnerable. If a large part of our mind is unconscious, how do we know that religious feelings, feelings of peace, harmony, the unity and significance of the universe, come from outside us, from God, or from inside us, from long-forgotten childhood memories or fantasies? Or is the distinction, in fact, not a real one? An analyst like Jung was capable of writing a great deal about the necessity of religion and about his conviction of God's existence. But "existence" for Jung meant "psychic existence". God, for him, existed as a psychological fact. As an analyst he could say nothing, and was not concerned, about whether this psychological fact corresponded with any objective reality.

Jung's limitation illustrates the limitation of psychology as a whole. Because it deals solely with what goes on in our minds, it can never make pronouncements about the reality or otherwise of the things we think about. It analyses the processes of our thinking, not the objects of our thought. Of course, the two are not entirely separate. Psychologists have to make assumptions about what is real, in order to decide what is normal and what is abnormal thinking. It is not psychological expertise, but commonsense, which tells them that pink elephants are unlikely to be encountered on the walls of public houses; and therefore they can safely conclude that those who see them are hallucinated. But the judgments they have to make are not always as straightforward as this. Anyone who has encountered a person suffering from a completely worked-out system of paranoiac delusions knows how horribly convincing they can seem. And when a system of beliefs is shared among a large number of people over a very long period of time, who is to judge, on psychological evidence alone, what is delusion and what is truth?

The application of this to religion is obvious. Psychology can analyse the processes of religious thought. It can show us from where we derive some of our religious images, and how experience moulds the shape of our beliefs. But it cannot tell us whether or not our religion is a response to any spiritual reality, unless it has already decided beforehand whether or not such a spiritual reality exists. Freud *had* decided beforehand. He believed that religion was the enemy of science, and that science was the only road to knowledge. Therefore, for him, it was inevitable that religion should appear as a psychological aberration; and to trace its roots in childhood was a sufficient reason for dismissing it.

If Christianity were based solely on private religious experiences, on personal intuitions and inspirations, the psychological study of its origins would be of great, perhaps decisive, importance. But Christianity is not simply a matter of private inspiration. Christians claim that their faith is an attempt to answer perfectly reasonable questions about the nature and purpose of the universe, the meaning of existence, and the life, death and resurrection of Jesus Christ. Religious experience does not exist in a vacuum in which individuals manufacture fantasies out of their childhood hopes and fears. It is a way of interpreting experience as God-given, which has evolved through thousands of years among communities of people who have continually tested and revised their interpretations in the light of the facts of their day. The writers of the Bible were continually rubbing the noses of their readers in what had actually happened; their faith only survived and grew as it was justified by events. Not all events justified it. There are times when we find them hanging on in bewilderment and frustration. The most that any believer ought to claim is that there is enough historical evidence to make faith reasonable. But the fact that these historical claims are made at all is sufficient reason for not allowing psychology to have the last word.

When this basic point is made, however, it remains true that psychological analysis can throw a flood of light on the contents of religious belief. To see how religiosity can be based on a fear of freedom and a failure of love, how it can build up a protective mechanism of rules and regulations, is to understand why Jesus was so uncompromising in his attack on the Pharisees, who had done this very thing. The same insight helps us to understand Paul's insistence on "justification by faith"; we break out of the strait-jacket of religiosity and self-justification, not by our own exertions, but by opening ourselves to the love which inwardly we have been rejecting.

Even the doctrine of the fatherhood of God, which superficially seems such an obvious candidate for psychological exposure, can be illuminated and purified rather than destroyed. There is a clear relationship between a person's image of his human father, and his image of God. In the days when fathers were stern autocrats ruling over Victorian households, God was likewise regarded mainly as a Holy Judge, much concerned with morals, ruling men and the universe with inflexible laws. In these days of amiable and rather ineffective fathers, ruled often by their wives, popular religion sees God as vaguely benevolent, nice to have around even though He doesn't do much. On a much deeper level, it is often possible to see how a person's fear of God, or belief that God is a vengeful tyrant, or that God doesn't care, or that He doesn't exist, can be linked with childhood experiences of dominance or indifference by one or other of his parents.

Christian analysts who try to distinguish what they would call "false images of God" from true ones, make it clear that to call God "father" can be disastrously misleading to those for whom the word "father" implies rejection, misery or tyranny. God is like a perfect father, they say; all actual human fathers are less than perfect; they fail their children in one way or another; and the children bear the scars of their failures when they come to think about God.

But where does this idea of a perfect father come from, if it is not in some way derived from our ideas about the fatherhood of God? And where did the Victorian paterfamilias derive his image of himself if he did not in some sense think of it as a rôle given him by God? Perhaps an easy-going modern parent is less inclined to justify his attitude by referring to the benevolence of God; but I suspect that his beliefs, or lack of them, in fact influence his conception of what it is to be a father. What I am suggesting is that there is a two-way traffic between beliefs about human fatherhood and the fatherhood of God, and that we find the two related, not because one is a mere reflection of the other, but because they have developed side by side.

This is not to deny that there are very large elements in the notion of human fatherhood which depend on natural instinct, economic necessity and social convention. But there is an ideal element in it, which in ancient societies was summed up in a religiously based belief in a father's rights, and in our modern society resides in a much vaguer sense of the privileges and responsibilities of fatherhood. Only when this element is ignored does it become convincing to claim that the notion of the father-hood of God is derived from human fatherhood, and nothing more.

We can make the same point from the reverse direction. God is called "father" in many religions; in primitive religions, especially, there was often thought to be an almost physical relationship between God and the tribe. We might have ex-pected Biblical religion to show a gradual transformation and purification of the image from these crude beginnings, as men's ideas about God became higher, and their concept of parent-hood more like our own. But this is not what we find at all.

In the Old Testament the idea of the fatherhood of God barely exists. There are one or two references to the "sons of God" in some of the most primitive (and pagan) sections of Genesis and Job. Otherwise there are only a handful of references in the prophetic books (e.g. Hosea 11: 1), where the point is being made that Israel is called to a unique and special relationship with God, as has been shown by God's acts of deliverance throughout her history. The basis of the idea of fatherhood, in other words, is historical fact, not wishful thinking.

When we turn to the New Testament we do not find, as is so often thought, a lot of vague general and comforting statements about God as the father of all mankind. The overwhelming majority of references use the word to describe God as the father of Jesus, and the context is usually the same as that of the Old Testament references—God's acts of deliverance in history, now reaching their fulfilment in Jesus. (In technical theological language—the references are primarily "Messianic".) Only secondarily does the New Testament teach that because Jesus is uniquely related to God, so the disciples of Jesus can come to share a similar, though less intimate, kind of relationship, and hence call God "father" too (see, for example, Luke 10: 21– 22). Paul called this relationship sonship "by adoption" (e.g. Romans 8: 15); Christians call God father because they belong to the only Son of the father, Jesus.

Apart from these uses of father–son imagery, which are very numerous indeed, references to God as the father of all mankind are almost non-existent (Matthew 5: 45 is a possible example). In fact, so strong is the belief that the image of God as father derives from its special use by Jesus, rather than from any general feelings about God's benevolence or wishful thinking about a Divine protector, that in the Epistle to the Ephesians we find it directly asserted that human fatherhood finds its meaning in Divine fatherhood, and not vice versa. After summarising the gospel of God's deliverance in Christ, the writer goes on, "For this cause I bow my knees unto the father from whom all fatherhood in heaven and on earth is named" (Ephesians 3: 14–15). We need not take this as a literal account of the way in which the word "father" got its meaning. The point is the same one that I was trying to make earlier; namely that there is a two-way traffic between beliefs about human fatherhood, and the fatherhood of God.

Such a long aside on Biblical thought may seem out of place in a chapter on psychology. But the field covered by psychology is so vast, and psychological theories are so varied, that it seemed best to concentrate on one particular Christian image which has been the object of much psychological analysis, and which seems to lend itself so invitingly to a process of psychological debunking. I hope this aside has shown that the situation is more complex than it seems at first sight.

Psychological analysis can do valuable work for Christianity in bringing to the surface the unconscious associations which religious images often have for us. It can expose unworthy and childish longings. It can show that what sometimes appear to be religious problems are not religious at all, but psycho-patho-logical. It can make us very much more tolerant of one another, when we recognise the maze of mixed motives, hidden fears and irrational prejudices inside each of us.

But these achievements, important though they are, do not give psychologists the right to make final pronouncements about the origin and validity of the great Christian images. These images have their own history within the Bible, and their own points of anchorage in objective facts. Their psychological colouring may be of great significance. A Christian need not deny this; in fact he should welcome it for the insight which it brings. All he needs to claim is that behind the images there is something real to be coloured. In the case of this particular image of fatherhood, the point of anchorage in objective fact is the language used by Jesus to describe his own relationship with God. If this leads to a comforting belief about our own relation-ship with God, the belief is not to be discredited merely on the grounds that it is comforting.

Chapter 14

THE BOUNDARIES OF NATURE

An Indian teacher was once describing to a pupil how the world is supported on the back of a giant Indian elephant. "And what supports the elephant?" asked his pupil. "The elephant is standing on the back of a giant tortoise," came the reply. "And what's the tortoise standing on?" The teacher said he hadn't thought about that, and would have to consider it.

Years later a science teacher, perhaps in that same school, was describing to a pupil how matter is made up of little particles called atoms, and how the whole varied structure of all the material things in the world can be explained in terms of the combination of these particles. "And what are atoms made of?" asked his pupil. "Atoms are made of even smaller particles called electrons and protons and neutrons, and possibly many others besides," the teacher replied. "And what are electrons and protons and neutrons made of?" The teacher said that no-body knew the answer to that one yet, but he was sure they would discover it soon.

Perhaps the comparison is unfair. However, at least the stories are alike in this respect: both teachers were trying to explain the unknown in terms of the known; their explanations pointed their pupils to objects they were already familiar with in the world of nature. It is not impossible to imagine giant elephants and tortoises. And we know what particles are; so we think we know what very, very minute particles are like. But the trouble with this kind of explanation is that the explanation itself demands explanation, and so on and so on, until the teacher has gone mad or the pupil has died of old age.

Primitive scientific explanations are generally of this kind. How can human spermatozoa develop and grow into highly intricate human babies? Because they are human bodies in miniature already! Early enthusiasts with the microscope even declared that they could see "little men" going about their business in seminal fluid.

What is the structure of the universe? A gigantic machine

held together by the same forces which determine the structure of man-made machines.

What is an atom? A miniature solar system, so we were once taught. And our minds went off into fantastic speculations about whether there could be another whole world of creatures inside each of these tiny systems.

The only way of breaking out of an infinite series of explanations of the elephant–tortoise variety is to see that we cannot have a satisfactory explanation for anything, unless it is different in kind from the thing we are explaining. Elephants and tortoises cannot explain why the earth stays up in space, because they themselves are part of the phenomenon to be explained. Talk about life forces, vital spirits, etc., cannot explain the phenomenon of life, because they are only an alternative, and vaguer, way of describing it. The ultimate method of advance for biology has been by breaking out of biological concepts into physics and chemistry. The ultimate method of advance for chemistry has been by interpreting its characteristic concepts, like valency, in terms of physics. But where is physics to advance? Where ought it to break out, if its explanations are really to explain, and not just lead us into an infinite regress of smaller and smaller ultimate particles?

I have been discussing in a general way a dilemma which is much more usually discussed under some such heading as "The Revolution in Physics" or "Whither Astronomy?". Physicists and astronomers are peculiarly exposed to this dilemma because theirs are subjects which, more than any others, operate on the boundaries of nature—the boundaries of the very large and the very small.

Most popular books on astronomy eventually lead us to the point where our minds reel under the impact of unimaginable numbers and distances. They raise the problem of space and time, of whether one can extrapolate these infinitely in both directions. Had the universe a beginning; or does it have an infinite series of fresh beginnings in the creation of hydrogen atoms? Is there an upper limit to velocity? What, in fact, does velocity mean if there is no fixed point in the universe from which it can be measured? All these questions give one a feeling of standing at the edge of the known world, while one searches for concepts to fill the gaping hole in one's imagination. This is perhaps why astronomers are especially prone to add a chapter on religion, either for or against it, at the end of their books.

The same is true of physics. A really searching enquiry into the structure of matter leads to the same bafflement of the imagination. Most people nowadays have at least heard of the paradoxes of quantum physics: the dual nature of light, now seeming to be waves, now particles; the indeterminacy principle, which sets a limit on our powers of describing an elementary particle—we can know the position or the velocity of an electron accurately, but not both; the statistical nature of the laws describing radiation, whereby we can know accurately, say, the rate of radioactive decay of plutonium, but are completely ignorant about why any particular atom should emit radiation at any particular moment. Nuclear physics, too, is rapidly adding to the number of unimaginable entities as the list of elementary particles grows larger; at the time of writing there are already hundreds, none of which seems to be a compound of any of the others. The biggest problem confronting theoretical physicists is to try to find a way of reducing this proliferation of elementary particles to some common denominator.

Like modern astronomy, modern physics has been used extensively by religious and philosophical writers to show that science is not so hostile to religion as once was thought. Some writers have suggested that the indeterminacy principle leaves scope for free will in an otherwise deterministic universe. There has been much talk about the breakdown of the Newtonian world view; and it has even been claimed that the church was right after all in its opposition to Galileo, because the theory of relativity has shown that whether the earth is stationary and the sun moves, or vice versa, all depends on one's point of view.

I have deliberately mentioned these modern developments of physics and astronomy only cursorily, because I think the use made of them by religious writers is very often wrong-headed, and gives the false impression that the sudden discovery of some new scientific facts has radically altered the religious situation. If this were so, then the discovery of a few more facts might alter the situation again.

The truth, as I see it, is that these discoveries have merely brought to the surface philosophical problems, which were inherent in science from the very start. Therefore it is best to discuss them in general terms, rather than become too enmeshed in scientific details.

In Chapter 3 we saw how physics set off on the road mapped out by Galileo. A distinction was drawn between the primary and secondary qualities of objects, and only the primary qualities—weight, distance and number—were considered to belong to the objects as such. Every other quality, it was thought, could eventually be explained in terms of these, and of the mind's powers of interpretation. Colour, for instance, came to be seen as a quality of mental experience conditioned by vibrations of a certain frequency. As physics advanced, the list of primary qualities was altered to fit the new facts; the concept of electric charge was a notable addition. But still, basically, the list was thought to consist of qualities familiar to us in our ordinary experience.

But this process could not go on indefinitely. One cannot explain the properties of matter by selecting some of those properties and explaining everything else in terms of them. Elephants may support a great deal of weight; but they cannot carry the whole world, because they themselves are part of it.

Modern physics has reached the point at which the basic properties of matter have been reduced to four—electric charge, mass, lifetime and spin. The strange variety of elementary particles can all be described in terms of these. If there is to be any unifying hypothesis to explain why there is this variety of particles with these charges, masses, etc., the hypothesis itself cannot make use of these four properties. But what else is there? We seem to pass right out of the realm of ordinary experience. And this is why modern physics seems so baffling. We are quite unable to form any mental picture of the basic stuff of which matter is formed; it was difficult enough trying to imagine electrons which behaved sometimes as if they were waves and sometimes as if they were particles; it seems impossible to imagine something which has no familiar properties at all.

This does not mean, however, that physicists are as baffled as laymen. Physicists do not need to worry so much about the unimaginability of what they are discussing, because for all practical purposes they can describe it quite adequately in mathematical terms. Mathematics is a device which enables us to dispense with mental pictures; it enables us to discuss the relationship between things with complete precision, without forcing us to say what the things are. It can give an exact and comprehensible form to apparent contradictions. The indeterminacy principle, for example, does not mean that at a certain point physics relapses into vagueness; it means that the equations describing the behaviour of elementary particles contain probability functions, and therefore do not have unique solutions. The most we can claim to know is the statistical probability of finding a particle in a particular place, not its precise location.

Some people have been so impressed by the power of mathematics to explain these abstruse physical phenomena, that they have talked about "ultimate reality" as mathematical, or even about God as a mathematician. But this is nonsense. Mathematics is a device which enables us to manipulate symbols or quantities very much more conveniently than in any other way. It enables us to express relationships between physical quantities which could not be expressed in words or images. I have already described in Chapter 2 how advances in science have been closely linked with advances in mathematics, and how mathematical explanations fulfil the scientific ideal. But mathematics is a device—not "ultimate reality"; it describes relationships—not things.

Thus, although physicists can do their work without straining their imaginations to picture the things they are describing, the fact that these cannot be pictured is not unimportant. It raises in a specially sharp way the question, what is a scientific explanation? What are science's claims to tell us about the nature of "reality"? Is science itself no more than a device for handling certain aspects of our experience, rather than a gateway to the truth? Perhaps the most important philosophical consequence of the revolution in physics has been to make scientists take a much harder and more critical look at what they are doing.

One way of describing the revolution is by saying that it has brought to the fore the rôle of the observer in science. Classical physics was built on the assumption that the world consists of objects, which exist entirely independently of those who are observing them, and whose behaviour can be studied with complete objectivity and described with complete precision. To a large extent this assumption still holds good; the world of ordinary objects can still be studied in this way.

But when we start dealing with the very large or the very

small, complications arise. In the study of matter we seem no longer to be dealing with "objective realities" in the sense in which ordinary perception gives meaning to the word "object". The behaviour of the things we study depends on the questions we ask about them; ask certain kinds of question of an electron, and it shows its nature as a wave; ask other questions and it shows its nature as a particle; ask questions about its velocity, and you have to give up the possibility of knowing its position; and so on. Nor are these merely human or technical limitations; they are inherent in the phenomena themselves. Just as it is impossible to find out what another person is thinking without forcing him to crystallise his thoughts in one form or another, so, in the words of von Weizsäcker, "We force the atom, as it were, to tell us its properties in an inadequate language. . . ." And so the whole story can never be told at the same time. The story we elicit depends on the question we, as observers, have asked.

This is not, of course, to imply that modern physics is "subjective". The results of physical experiments do not depend on what is going on in the minds of individual physicists. The claim still holds good that *any* physicist should, in theory, be able to obtain the same results. But what cannot be left out of the account of these phenomena is the fact that they are being observed; it does not matter whether the experiments were done by Professor X or Y or Z; they were being observed by *somebody*. And this is an obvious truth about science in general which has far too frequently been ignored. As Heisenberg put it, "Quantum theory reminds us of the old wisdom that when searching for harmony in life one must never forget that in the drama of existence we are ourselves both players and spectators".

The same point is brought home to us by the theory of relativity. This began at the opposite end of the scale, in the study of very large velocities, approaching the velocity of light. Its most familiar conclusion is that there is no fixed frame of reference in space and time. There is no set of Cartesian co-ordinates, of the kind presupposed by Newtonian physics, in relation to which times and positions and velocities can be plotted on an absolute scale. All motion is relative to the person who is observing it (hence the name of the theory); and therefore time and position are relative too. We can only measure these quantities in relation to a particular frame of reference which we ourselves have chosen. As in the case of quantum theory, the rôle of the observer cannot be left out; and this is not a technical or human limitation; it is inherent in the nature of things.

A few sentences can hardly give any indication of the beauty and profundity and revolutionary impact of these theories. But since the vast majority of the human race will never be able to understand them, there is something to be said for trying to express very simply the difference they should make to our understanding of science. To stress the rôle of the observer in science may not seem a very exciting conclusion; but as I hope to show in the next chapter, it has considerable implications.

We can perhaps picture the physical world like this. Immediately around us is the world of familiar things, to which we give the name "objects", and which provide us with our criteria for deciding what is real and what is not. This is why philosophers talk so insistently about chairs and tables when they want to describe physical reality; chairs and tables belong to this familiar world. Science had its great initial successes in explaining the familiar world by showing how its parts fitted together and reacted on one another; and its explanations, whether fully understood or not, have sunk deeply into modern people's imaginations.

But now science has pushed out beyond the boundaries of familiarity, and a different picture has emerged, a picture whose implications are far more difficult to imagine. In this region, at the boundaries of nature, the criteria of objectivity break down; we cannot extrapolate from the familiar world to this boundary world without recognising the contribution which we ourselves make to our descriptions of it. The scientific ideal of the limitless extension of objective knowledge is frustrated. An element of arbitrariness and choice enters in.

The imaginative impact of this new picture of the world has not been nearly so clear-cut as the old. We saw in Chapter 11 how some religious writers have welcomed it as heralding the final collapse of a naïve materialism, as setting scientific knowledge firmly within its limitations. Others, however, have passed from materialism, not to religion, but to agnosticism; for them the word "relativity" has spread its shadow, not only over physics, but over all knowledge and over all human obligations.

The crucial question is whether all knowledge must find its

THE BOUNDARIES OF NATURE

model and its basis in scientific knowledge, and so share its limitations. Or whether religion can make good its claim to speak of things which transcend scientific knowledge. This is the question which must concern us in the remaining chapters of this book.

Chapter 15

MAPS

Imagine what it would be like never to have seen a map of Great Britain. We might have explored the whole coastline, and visited the most important towns; we might know the distances between them, and even have formulae for calculating their positions relative to one another. But there would still be a sense in which it could be said that we did not know what Great Britain was like unless we had seen or drawn a map of it.

The converse is true as well. We may often have looked at maps of the U.S.A. but, unless we have actually been there, our knowledge of it will be very superficial. Maps are no substitute for on-the-spot experience. But they can co-ordinate our experiences, and the experiences of others, in a way which gives genuinely new insight. Maps reveal relationships between places, which we might never have seen otherwise, or could have discovered only by the most laborious calculations; they give us a guide for an infinite number of possible journeys; they extend our knowledge without necessarily increasing our stock of information. When we draw a plan of our own home, we may think we know every nook and cranny of it; but the plan gives us a new way of seeing it all. When we are travelling, a map enables us to predict what we shall see when we reach a certain place. Preliminary maps of unexplored territory show the limits of our knowledge, and indicate the kind of country to be expected.

Maps, in short, behave very much like scientific theories. A scientific theory shows the relationship between different bits of empirical experience. It does not add any information, but it may reveal things or suggest the existence of things which cannot be seen or measured directly, just as many of the shapes on maps cannot be seen directly. In its day, a theory like the theory of gravitation provided a genuinely new insight; it co-ordinated a large quantity of observations into a coherent and satisfying whole; it gave a basis for understanding an infinite number of particular experiences; it made possible all sorts of predictions which could be verified by experiment. A tentative hypothesis, like a preliminary map, shows the limits of knowledge by fixing a few of the facts to be explained, and indicating the kind of future exploration which will be needed.

We can extend the comparison even further. Sometimes it happens that advances in technique make it possible to observe directly things whose existence previously has only been inferred. The shape of the coastline of Great Britain can now be seen directly from a satellite. In the same way, molecules, whose existence was at first inferred as part of chemical theory, can now be photographed directly through an electron microscope. This sort of direct confirmation suggests that the shapes on our maps and the things inferred by science are not to be dismissed as arbitrary constructions, mere concepts which have no physical reality. Nevertheless, there *is* an arbitrary element in map-making, just as there is in science. The form of a map, its co-ordinates, scale, conventional signs, etc., depend on the arbitrary choice of the map-maker, just as scientific scales of measurement and concepts like "specific heat" depend upon agreement between scientists. This does not make maps and theories "subjective"; it merely emphasises that they are maps and theories, and hence human constructions, and not the things themselves.

A map is a completely self-consistent whole, just as a scientific theory is. There should be no gaps or awkward joins or embarrassing extra features on maps, which do not correspond with things actually there on the ground. In the same way, the mathematics of a mathematical theory make it rigid and exact; there is no scope for fudging the answer. Within the framework of the theory of gravitation the inverse square law always applies, and we cannot pretend that the formula is $\frac{MM^1}{d^{2.1}}$ if that happens to fit the facts better; we have to look for some additional factor. Though the *theory* may be rigid and exact, its application to a particular set of circumstances always carries the proviso "other things being equal". And in practice they seldom are; which is why scientific experiments are generally very much more difficult to perform than they seem when they are simply read about in a book. And finding one's way with a map may be more difficult than it seems too. In terms of what it is trying to show, the map may be exact and consistent. But the varied features of the ground do not fit completely into the map-makers' categories. How secondary is a secondary road, or how

ruined is a ruined castle, or how tall is a wood? Anybody who
has driven miles across country to see a small heap of stones
calling itself a castle knows that, although maps may be accurate, it is often difficult to know exactly what to expect.

Some of these difficulties can be removed by using different
kinds of maps with different scales and different purposes—historical atlases, physical atlases, rainfall maps, etc.
These correspond to the different scientific theories within a
hierarchy, or to the different sciences themselves; there are highly
general theories like the theory of gravitation, and more particular applications of it, like the law of acceleration of freely
falling bodies on earth. Different sciences select different
features of experience for study, and use their own characteristic concepts.

In all these ways the analogy between maps and scientific
theories holds fairly exactly; and it provides what I believe to be
the most illuminating account of what science claims to do. I
now propose to extend the analogy to take into account some
of the facts discussed in the last chapter. The business of extending analogies is always dangerous, but provided we are
aware of the dangers, it need not necessarily be misleading.

A map is a two-dimensional representation of a three-
dimensional reality. For many of the purposes for which maps
are used, the third dimension does not matter very much, and
where it does matter it can be represented by special devices,
such as contour lines. The lack of a third dimension only becomes a serious problem when the area covered by the map is
either very small or very large.

In areas of the size covered by most ordinary maps, vertical
distances are negligible in comparison with horizontal distances.
But as the area becomes smaller and smaller, vertical distances
become relatively more important, and a single two-dimensional
map becomes less and less satisfactory. The best way of drawing a plan of a two-storey house, for example, is to draw two
pictures side by side. In terms of the analogy, this may correspond with the impossibility of using a single model to describe
an electron; at least two models are necessary, waves and
particles.

Maps of very large areas run into difficulties caused by the
curvature of the earth. Like the vertical element we have just
been considering, this is a factor which affects every map at

every point. But in maps of the kind we use for everyday travelling, its effect is negligible. It is only when we try to represent a large part of the world that it becomes important, and geographers are forced to use different projections, all of which

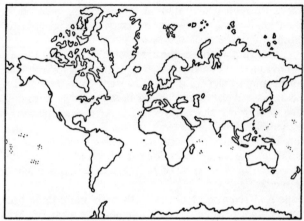

Figure 3.   The World.   Mercator's Projection

are in some respects inaccurate and unsatisfactory. Mercator's projection leads to obvious and ludicrous distortion at the edges, and would be highly unsatisfactory if one lived in Siberia or Greenland. Whereas the Interrupted Mollweide's Homolographic projection avoids serious distortion of land masses, but leaves those strange chasms in the middle of the sea.

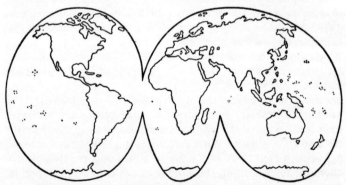

Figure 4.   Interrupted Mollweide's Homolographic Projection

In terms of our analogy, these distortions, and the apparently nonsensical behaviour of one or other part of any map of the world, may correspond with the apparently strange behaviour of objects at the limits of space. And the map-makers' different projections may remind us of the different frames of reference through which alone it is possible to investigate the universe, and which the theory of relativity has brought to our attention.

I do not want to press the resemblance between these properties of maps and particular scientific theories too far, because one of the main points of the last chapter was to show that these particular discoveries have simply brought to the fore complications concerning the nature of scientific explanation which were there from the start. Nevertheless the comparison may be useful, because at the boundaries of map-making, as at the boundaries of nature, limitations in our methods become obvious, which in the world of ordinary experience might have been overlooked.

Maps and scientific theories both have limitations because they are attempts to describe an immensely complicated reality in inadequate terms. They are both human constructions, in the sense that they express, in terms agreed among human beings, the answers to questions which human beings have framed. Good maps and good theories may be perfectly adequate for the purposes for which they were designed. But if too much is claimed for them, then distortions and oversimplification begin to appear.

Throughout this book we have noted occasions in the advance of science when the pressure of religious and philosophical questions has begun to make itself felt. In the study of life, for example, we saw how there can be an awareness of living things which makes a purely physico-chemical description of them seem very thin and artificial. The temptation to which vitalists succumbed was to claim that there were gaps in the physico-chemical map which the mechanists had overlooked. The mechanists replied, quite correctly, that there were no gaps; their maps covered the whole ground, and vitalists were looking for a will o' the wisp. What both sides might have been able to agree on is that there is a sense of strain in a purely physico-chemical account of life, because we know life also from within, by being alive; we know it in depth; there is an extra dimension in our understanding of it. The analogy of the extra dimension enables us to see how scientific explanations can be complete in relation to what they set out to do, and yet can leave out extremely important realms of experience.

The analogy of the extra dimension may help us also to make some sense of the elephant-tortoise dilemma posed in the last chapter. The problem was that our categories of explanation are derived from the familiar world of things; and therefore when pushed to the limit they cannot explain the world of things. We cannot explain the properties of particles in terms of smaller particles, and so on *ad infinitum*. Somehow or other we have to reach through to a different type of explanation, or open up an extra dimension in our thinking. Some philosophers have suggested that the ultimate category of explanation ought to be the notion of "events" rather than "things"; this sort of idea may have important future uses in theoretical physics, but it does not escape the basic dilemma, because the majority of "events" within our experience happen to "things".

There is an ancient argument for the existence of God which makes use of this dilemma; it argues that the only ultimate explanation of things is to be found in a different kind of reality altogether; and this reality it identifies with God. The argument is somewhat out of favour nowadays because it seems to beg too many questions. But the dilemma from which it starts is a real one. And if the analogy of the extra dimension carries any weight at all, it might help to give a mental picture of the sort of relationship which God bears to the world.

But this is perhaps to read too much out of the analogy at this stage. I do not want to suggest that the third dimension missing from our scientific maps can simply be identified with God, or the supernatural realm, or anything equivalent. The sole purpose of the analogy is to show how scientific explanations can in one sense be complete, yet still leave a great deal to to be said.

Before leaving the analogy, however, I want to raise a further question; what is it that scientific theories are mapping? What are they maps *of*?

In Chapter 11 this question was touched on in discussing the relation between pure science and technology. There are some who would deny that science is any more than a practical way of getting things done; it helps us to manipulate nature, and need not concern itself with questions about ultimate reality. In other words, scientific maps are convenient guides, and no more; they may be imposing regularities on nature which do not in fact exist. Nietzsche, as we saw, believed this to be the case. Science, for him, was man's attempt to impose order on a chaotic world. "The will to truth is *merely* the longing for a *stable world*."

Here is an example of a less extreme form of the same attitude—a point of view known as conceptualism: "A scientific law is a means of correlating experiences. And the pattern to which it refers is a pattern built around concepts. There is no law of gravitation except in our own minds as we try to comprehend the falling stone; there is no electron except in our imagination as we seek to understand the behaviour of the wireless valve; there is no radioactive nucleus unless it be a creature of our own invention, conceived and born that we may the better make sense of flashes of light on a fluorescent screen. . . ." In other words, scientific theories map our experience of the ordinary world, a world modified maybe by experiment, a world containing dials and pointers and fluorescent screens, but the contents of the theories, particles like electrons, are not real in the sense in which the dials and pointers are real. This is a view of the nature of scientific theories which obviously fits very well into modern physics; we avoid the dilemmas caused by reaching out from the ordinary world towards the boundaries of nature, by never in fact leaving the ordinary world. We stay with our dials and our pointers and simply explain how they behave.

But will this do? If it is possible to *see* molecules through an electron microscope, then we can have just as good evidence of their existence as of the existence of chairs and tables. But if molecules are objects rather than concepts, what are we to say about atoms and electrons? Does something become merely a useful concept below a certain critical size? Can we have objects (molecules) made up of smaller objects (atoms) made up of concepts (protons, neutrons and electrons)? The dilemma cannot be solved by going to the opposite extreme and calling electrons objects, because, as we have already seen, they do not behave like objects in the usual sense of the word.

Conceptualism, I believe, is an oversimplification. It avoids this sort of problem by glossing over the fact that we cannot draw a rigid dividing line between objects and concepts. In the early years of science there was a tendency to make precisely the opposite mistake, to imagine that everything which scientists postulated or described was "real" in the full objective sense of the word. The truth seems to lie somewhere in between. When we use the words "reality", "objects", "what ultimately exists", etc., we tend to give them many different levels of meaning. We start, as I have repeatedly said, from the world of ordinary experience; and then we use the words to apply to other realms of experience, extending them by analogy, without always realising what we are doing. There is an analogy between the existence of chairs and the existence of electrons, but the word "existence" does not mean precisely the same in both contexts. The same point is worth remembering when talking about the existence of God; when some modern theologians make startling remarks like "God doesn't exist" they are drawing attention to the dangers of a naïve use of the word "exist", in much the same way that conceptualism has done for science.

The right way of framing a question about the existence of electrons is not "Do electrons exist?" but "How far is the use of the word existence helpful or misleading in our attempts to describe them?" Questions in this form enable us to answer that our scientific maps are maps of something which is "really there"; but we can only know about this reality in terms of analogies drawn from the world of ordinary experience; and these become more and more misleading as we push our investigations to the limit. There is a parallel in this with the questions asked in Chapter 7 about the nature of life. I suggested there a question of the form "What are the most useful terms in which to try to understand living creatures?", and argued that answers solely in terms of physics and chemistry became more and more misleading as our investigations were pushed to the limit; they need to be supplemented by answers drawn from our own experience of being alive.

It might be that what the physical sciences need are similar sets of supplementary answers. Maps are inadequate representations of an immensely complicated reality; and part of that reality is ourselves. We do not derive our notion of existence only from the existence of material objects around us; we know about existence directly by virtue of the fact that we exist. And we know ourselves neither as objects nor as concepts. So it is not surprising that when we try to push the whole of reality into one or the other category, we find ourselves confronted with some apparently insoluble dilemmas.

Chapter 16

THE SCIENTIFIC ATTITUDE

In the late 1940s I was working in a laboratory where two of the research workers were members of the Communist party. Ordinarily this made no difference whatever to their attitude to their work. But in those years a controversy arose in Russian scientific circles which deeply shook the scientific world as a whole and caused a conflict in the minds of these British Communists, very like the early conflicts between science and religion.

The trouble was caused by a leading Russian geneticist, Lysenko, who in the name of Marxist dogma threw overboard the whole of orthodox genetics, with its basic premise that hereditary characteristics are stable and cannot be modified by changes of environment. Any theory which presupposed innate differences between people or between plants was labelled fascist; it was a denial of dialectical materialism. Western genetics was "tainted with theism" (Mendel, its founder, was a priest). Lysenko's followers wrote of "the enormous social-class significance of our controversy".

Lysenko himself was a plant-breeder who had had some practical successes, and had managed to inspire Soviet farmers with a sense of what they could achieve, at a critical stage in the development of Soviet agriculture. He claimed that his revolutionary genetical theories were confirmed by experiment; but his results were, to say the least, dubious, and were presented with a mixture of rhetoric, wild assertion, denunciation and dogmatism, which were highly embarrassing to more orthodox scientists. The controversy only became important when the State took Lysenko's side, promoted him to the highest scientific positions in the country, and began a persecution campaign against his scientific opponents. Science in Russia became temporarily the servant of politics; the ominous claim was heard "All science is class science". And my communist colleagues suffered an acute conflict of loyalties.

The Lysenko controversy is now finished and forgotten, and Russian science is probably as free from political bias as any other science. The incident is worth recalling, however, because it brought out into the open, in a very striking way, the system of values on which science rests, and the sense of community which binds scientists together. Western scientists felt Lysenko's actions as a stab in the back; he had betrayed the scientific attitude, and in so doing had revealed the insecurity of its foundations.

Science rests on a system of values. A certain moral and intellectual integrity must be presupposed before it can ever begin. There must be a passionate concern about truth for its own sake. There must be a readiness to persevere, and a belief that the universe is intelligible, and therefore that the quest is worthwhile. All these are fairly obvious requirements, but the need for them explains why science cannot flourish in every kind of culture.

In addition to these basic values, there is a need for professional standards, and for an atmosphere of trust and mutual recognition among scientists. In theory any scientist ought to be able to verify any results claimed by another scientist, and one of the strengths of science is that this possibility should lift scientific conclusions above the level of personal considerations. But in practice this cannot and does not happen very much. Scientists rely on the names and reputations of well-known individual workers or laboratories. There is a general feeling that the truth will out eventually, as in the case of the exposure, after many years, of the Piltdown skull as a forgery. But this is a long, sometimes a very long, process. Where there is any large breakdown in mutual confidence the whole scientific structure is shaken.

Scientists form a community. As in most communities there are certain conditions of membership, forms of initiation and orthodoxies generally believed among its members. The majority of scientists become what they are by taking a science degree and then serving for a time in a laboratory under expert guidance. Occasionally very gifted amateurs enter the community some other way, but if they have no normal qualifications their results are treated with great suspicion until they have proved themselves and been vindicated by recognised authorities. The method of initiation includes becoming familiar with a large mass of orthodox scientific theory, as well as learning techniques, and developing the standards of criticism and accuracy demanded by rigorous scientific proof. These things do not come naturally; they have to be learnt, much as an art or skill is learnt. Members of the community are rightly critical of those who have not been through the necessary disciplines.

Sometimes orthodox theories are challenged by radically new ideas, and there is a period of confusion while it is decided whether the new ideas are scientific or not. This is not as easy as it sounds, because there is no simple criterion by which to decide. The new ideas may be based on factual evidence, gathered so far as one can tell in a genuinely scientific way; yet they may be so revolutionary in their consequences that the majority of scientists are unwilling to accept them. Freudian theory is a good example of a set of ideas which had to fight a stiff battle for recognition. Parapsychology, the study of telepathy, clairvoyance, precognition, etc., is an example of one which is still fighting. The factual evidence from card-guessing experiments may seem to some to be overwhelming proof of the existence of telepathy. But there are good and otherwise fairminded scientists who would rather claim that there is something grievously wrong with the experiments or with the statistics by which they are interpreted, than admit that something so odd and apparently anomalous as telepathy can occur.

How is one to decide? The history of science is full of stories of unlikely ideas which have eventually become accepted, and apparently likely ideas which have come to grief. In practice scientists maintain their balance in the face of new ideas by a certain broad conservatism, and it is by no means true that beautiful hypotheses are always slain by the first blow from ugly facts. There are countless examples of hypotheses which have been clung to in spite of the evidence, because scientists have felt in their bones that they were right, and which have eventually been vindicated.

There is, in short, a process of judgment involved in deciding what is scientific and what is not. Though many people have tried to describe exact criteria, none of these work as well as one would like. The elegance or simplicity of a hypothesis may be a guide to its truth, but it is not an infallible guide. Who is to decide what is elegant? And who is seriously going to claim that quantum theory is simple? The power of a hypothesis to predict future results is also extensively quoted as if this were the final criterion of its truth. But in the case of parapsychology it is a criterion which it is virtually impossible to apply. In fact, on the frontiers of knowledge, scientists rely on their own judgments about the inherent likeliness or unlikeliness of ideas, and these judgments are backed by all that they have learnt from their membership of the scientific community.

This emphasis on personal judgment and membership of a community draws attention to features of the scientific method which are often overlooked. There is a popular misconception of scientists as white-coated automata who, by applying certain well-defined principles of investigation with relentless efficiency, push back the frontiers of knowledge willy-nilly. But this is not what actually happens, except at a very low level of research. Even the phrase "scientific method" implies more standardisation than exists in practice. It is true that there are certain broad principles which apply to all scientific work—the making of preliminary hypotheses, the design of crucial experiments, the use of controls, etc. But there are no rules for making discoveries. When scientific results are written up in learned journals they are presented in a logical form which makes the process of discovery seem much more straightforward than it actually is. The impersonal language of a scientific paper often conceals an immense amount of personal skill and judgment, and long processes of trial and error. It is often true that the neater and more inevitable the final result appears to be, the greater was the personal skill needed to obtain it. And this is why not everybody can be a good scientist. Low-grade semi-automatic research can be done by anybody of reasonable intelligence, and it is to such research that the popular image of scientists tends to apply. But important discoveries are not made in this way; they are made only by people who have mastered a highly demanding art, and who are as creative as those who practise other branches of art.

Learning to be a scientist, being initiated into the scientific community, discovering how to handle scientific concepts, deciding how much weight to give to this or that consideration, or what nuance of interpretation is demanded here or there, has been compared with learning to be a Christian. W. G. Pollard, who is a leading American physicist as well as an Anglican clergyman, has recently written a fascinating book making the comparison in detail. The book sprang out of his own experience as an active member of two communities, scientific and religious, which he realised were operating on surprisingly similar principles. Knowledge, he claims, is always knowledge within a community, and only those who are prepared to be initiated, and to live and work within the community, can really penetrate the knowledge which its members claim to have. In an earlier chapter I referred to "the community of faith" as a way of describing those who produced the Bible, and I went on to claim that Christianity can only really be understood by those who are prepared to live and work within this same community of faith. If Pollard is right the need for such a community is not peculiar to Christianity, nor is faith a sophisticated kind of dishonesty demanded only by religion and entirely absent from science.

Pollard's book is welcome evidence, as is the growing tendency to stress the personal and creative element in scientific discovery, that the actual practice of science is now being discussed far more realistically than it used to be. Gone are the days when we could be content to draw a sharp dividing line between something called "the scientific method" and something else called "religious faith", as if one was entirely objective and impersonal, and the other was no more than fancy, prejudice or wishful thinking.

Nevertheless, although the contrast is not usually put as crudely as this, a disguised version of it still underlies many people's doubts about religion. It is all very well, they feel, to talk as in the last chapter about the limitations of scientific knowledge and about the philosophical problems which science forces upon our attention; it is all very well to talk about the scientific community and the values and insights which uphold it, and to compare it with the Christian community. But there remain basic differences between the scientific and religious attitudes to life which must not be glossed over. Every schoolboy, who in his science classes is urged to be as critical as he can be, and then in his divinity class is urged to have faith, feels the contrast for himself. I hope I have said enough in earlier chapters of this book to show what a subtle notion faith is, and how it need not necessarily be set in contrast to a critical approach to evidence. But still . . . science and religion as they are ordinarily presented to us feel very different from one another.

Science overwhelms us by its practical successes; it impresses us with its vast accumulation of knowledge, and the enormous areas of agreement among scientists.

Religion, on the other hand, can seem ineffective. Religions have divided people from one another, rather than united them. After thousands of years of thought there is still no agreement about the most fundamental articles of belief.

Science seems to gain its strength by its emphasis on objectivity, impartiality, the disinterested search for truth. The weaknesses of the various religions seem to stem from the element in them of passionate conviction; it is this which causes divisions; it is this which blinds men to the evidence of their senses; it is this which first makes religions effective, by rousing men to great heroism, but then makes them ineffective by cutting them off from their roots in reality.

Differences in subject matter account for part of this contrast. It is clearly much easier to study and reach some agreement on the behaviour of water-fleas, than to answer questions about the meaning and purpose of life. Science has won its victories by studying what can be studied, and asking questions which can be answered. And where questions have seemed too difficult, it has split them up or cut them down to size until it has found ways of answering them. Great questions about life are tackled scientifically by trying to answer innumerable lesser questions about the behaviour of living things.

As we have seen, however, repeatedly through this book, such an approach does not dispose of the kind of religious and philosophical problems posed by our own experience of being alive. Answers to these questions can only be in terms of personal insights and decisions. No matter how much Christians may stress the objective, historical aspects of their faith, and claim that their faith is the faith of an historical community, there remains a large personal element in it. Theology gives us a programme for personal action. To know God is not to add an extra card labelled "God" to our mental card index; it is to become a changed person. To a lesser degree, to learn science is to become a changed person also. But whereas in science the process of change is largely unconscious and often unrecognised, in religion it is paramount.

This stress on the element of personal insight and decision accounts for the bewildering variety of interpretations found even among members of the same Christian community. From one point of view this is a weakness; the modern world would listen to Christians much more respectfully if they all spoke with the same voice. But from another point of view it is a strength; the fact that so many interpretations are possible is the sign that they spring out of genuine personal insights, that theology is not a huge intellectual conspiracy, a pattern of thought imposed on people from outside with no roots in their personal lives. Variety, in other words, may be a sign of life, a sign that God can be found in every human circumstance; a sign that every intellectual statement about Him is inadequate, and tends to provoke its opposite.

To recognise the value of variety in this way is not necessarily to be in favour of theological anarchy. I wish to emphasise that personal insight is only one element in theology, and that there are aspects of theology which can be studied in just as impersonal and objective a manner as any scientist might desire. There are ways of distinguishing valid insights from idiosyncratic ones. Many popular interpretations of the Bible fly so much in the face of the conclusions of Biblical scholars, that for most purposes they are worthless. Yet often beneath superficial nonsense there is buried some genuine religious insight struggling for expression. Sects like Jehovah's Witnesses, which on the surface are committed to the most naïve and crude conceptions of religious warfare at the end of the world, may be meeting a need to believe that the struggle between good and evil really matters. They may also meet a less worthy need to feel self-righteous and to enjoy the pleasures of vengeance, and therein lies their danger. But the fact that a belief may be crude and even dangerous does not discredit such genuine religious insight as may lie beneath it.

Theology's concern with personal insight, therefore, inevitably leads to a strong contrast with science; but it is not an absolute contrast. There are sciences which demand almost as much personal involvement as theology. Psycho-analysis, for example, claims to be scientific in its approach, but the facts it discovers about the human psyche are very different from the kind of facts which occupy a physicist. The psycho-analytic truth about oneself can only be known by a process not unlike conversion; it is a personal truth which has to be accepted, not merely discovered. The analyst is not an impartial observer who learns the truth about his patient and then simply passes it on; he is more like a midwife who brings certain insights to birth in the process of reacting with his patient. So deeply is psycho-analysis committed to this kind of personal involvement that some have doubted whether it is a science at all. Freudianism, as we saw, had to struggle for a long time before it became part of scientific orthodoxy. This is because in many people's minds "science" means "physics"; the science in which it is easiest, and does least violence to the subject matter, to have a strictly objective, impersonal approach comes to stand for the whole of science; and everything else has to wait until it can conform to the standards which physics demands. When the position is put as crudely as this, the hopes of an understanding between science and theology are very slender indeed.

Suppose, however, we reject this very narrow view of science, and try to see what those who stress its objectivity and imper-sonality are trying to safeguard. Surely the aim of science is knowledge which can be universally agreed. Impersonality is valued as the only way of attaining this, and theology falls under suspicion for not having it.

But universal agreement is only possible in a community which shares the same aims and the same values. And within any community there are many levels of agreement. Even a community of physicists might begin to disagree when they discussed the aims and values which bound them together, de-spite the fact that their community depended on these very things. Explicit agreements are found most easily in the realms of greatest precision and least personal involvement; but there may be underlying agreements which are less easy to specify, and are immediately the subjects of furious argument when they are brought out into the open. These underlying agreements, though not capable of scientific analysis, are just as essential to the whole structure of knowledge as the more impressive parts where science has had its greatest successes.

It might follow, then, that the very possibility of impersonal scientific knowledge depends on hidden areas of agreement of a more personal kind. Just as at the end of the last chapter it was claimed that we cannot leave out of account in our description of reality the fact that we ourselves exist, so in our description of knowledge we have to remember that it is we, as persons, who know, and that we know, not in isolation, but as members of a community committed to certain ideals of knowledge. An anatomy of knowledge, if such a thing were possible, would have to make room for this element of communal commitment, and might discover a series of levels of knowledge with, say, theoretical physics at one extreme, and our knowledge of ourselves at the other. Psycho-analytic knowledge might come somewhere in the middle. At all levels the ideal of communal, universal, knowledge might be safeguarded; though obviously at the more personal levels such a universal ideal would need a great deal of working for.

I shall develop this view of knowledge further in the next chapter. But I hope it is already clear how both the scientific and the religious attitudes must have their place in a community's attempts to understand all levels of its experience.

Chapter 17

TYPES OF KNOWLEDGE

In his book, *Personal Knowledge*, Michael Polanyi draws a useful distinction between articulate and inarticulate knowledge. Science is the great example of articulate knowledge. The aim of science is to describe and explain the natural world as clearly and accurately as possible, using words or symbols whose meanings are precise and whose relationships can be expressed as far as possible mathematically. This highly articulate body of knowledge is so impressive that some have claimed it to be the only reliable kind of knowledge there is.

As I began to argue at the end of the last chapter, however, such a body of knowledge may presuppose another type of knowledge, whose existence may go unrecognised—what Polanyi calls "inarticulate knowledge". To bring this kind of knowledge out into the open may be the best way of challenging the claim that science holds the monopoly of truth.

A good example of inarticulate knowledge is our knowledge of a language. When we first start to learn a language, we are taught the appropriate words for chairs and trees and kings, etc., and it is easy to be misled into thinking that this is the way languages are built up—as if a vocabulary consisted of a list of precise words denoting particular objects; as if the growth of a language were a simple process of labelling.

But what is a chair? And when is a chair not a chair? There are all sorts of shapes and sizes and types of objects to which we apply the word "chair". The usefulness of the word depends partly on the fact that it is a vague one; and so is the word "tree". Both words relate together many different kinds of objects, and reveal connections which might otherwise not have been obvious. What is the relationship between an oak tree and a vine? To use the same word "tree" for both of them is an achievement; it is one of the first steps in botany; it implies an interpretation of experience; it involves a process very different from the mere labelling of objects which are obviously distinct.

The word "king" is a more complex example. What is it that makes us call one man a king and other men his subjects? The notion of kingship is highly sophisticated. There is a sense in which the word itself creates the idea. How can one have a king, with all the mystique which that implies, without a notion of kingship? And yet how can one have a notion of kingship unless one has seen a king? The description of language as a process of labelling is even more inappropriate in this instance than in the previous one.

The development of language is perhaps the greatest achievement of civilisation. Built into every language are thousands of years of experience and interpretation. The possibilities of different kinds of interpretation are shown by the fact that the words of different languages do not correspond with one another on a one-to-one basis. Theologians often point out the basic differences between Greek and Hebrew, and show how many of the characteristics of Jewish thought are subtly changed when they are expressed in Greek terminology. Those who learn Chinese become even more startlingly aware of the different outlooks on life which different languages can encourage.

To avoid the disadvantages of this built-in element of interpretation in all languages, scientists try to construct an artificial language of their own, deliberately designed to conform with their own scientific interpretations. This partly accounts for the use of, say, chemical symbols, or Latin names in botany. Some artificial words of this kind, like the words "electricity" and "mass", have come into general use, and scientists, in their turn, use very large numbers of ordinary words as well as their special ones. In fact, there is an interchange between scientific language and ordinary language, as there must be if science is to relate to the world of ordinary experience. Scientific language is an abstraction from the wider use of language—and presupposes it.

Some philosophers, notably the logical positivists, have been dissatisfied with this state of affairs, and have tried to make all language behave as if it were scientific language. There was the much publicised claim that statements which cannot be verified, as scientific statements are verified, must be meaningless. But few would now hold this extreme position. It has been recognised that human beings do in fact convey meaning to one another by using language in many different ways; and philosophy has to take account of this variety, rather than set up a rigid criterion of what is meaningful and what is not.

The use of a particular language is an art, learnt by living among those who speak it. Rules of grammar and syntax are attempts to formalise the use of it. But in any living language the knowledge of these alone is not enough in order to speak it well. There must be a feeling for the language, a fund of inarticulate knowledge built up by contact with it as a living thing.

A similar fund of inarticulate knowledge is presupposed in the practice of every art or skill. To hear Yehudi Menuhin trying to explain how he plays the violin is to realise that the essence of his art cannot be conveyed to an outsider at all. There are lesser skills in which an outsider might have a complete knowledge of the principles employed, and yet be unable to perform the skill itself. It is possible to read books on driving a motor car, and to have all the principles at one's fingertips, and yet not know how to drive; and conversely, a man might be a good driver while knowing very little about the theory of it.

There is a famous example of a lost skill quoted by Polanyi. Nobody today can make a Stradivarius violin. Existing Stradivarii have been subjected to the most minute analysis and copied in meticulous detail; but they are not as good as the originals. Possibly Stradivarius himself may not have understood how he did it; nevertheless, in another sense, he *knew* how to make violins, as nobody else before or since. Craftsmanship is mostly inarticulate knowledge, transmitted by means of apprenticeship; like language it depends on the existence of a living tradition. The tradition can always be broken, and the knowledge lost.

A third example of inarticulate knowledge is our knowledge of ourselves and other people. I have already discussed this in Chapter 12, and claimed that we do not know ourselves and each other by deducing our existence from observed facts. Our knowledge of ourselves presupposes human society; and so it presupposes a recognition of other human beings as basically like ourselves. And only on these presuppositions is language possible; and only by using language can we indulge in rational thought.

Our first awarenesses, I have claimed, are of our involvement in a highly complex personal situation. Only gradually do we begin to analyse this situation, to distinguish ourselves from other people, to separate subject and object, and to think of the world as made up of a lot of separate and nameable things. This is the complete opposite of what Locke believed to be the case when he wrote: " I say then that we have knowledge of our own existence by intuition; of the existence of God by demonstration; and of other things by sensation." Writing in the heyday of Newtonian science, he was unconsciously taking scientific knowledge as his model, without realising that this presupposes a great deal of previous interpretation. Behind the neat parcelling-up of experience, which seemed so natural to him, lay a long history of reflection and refinement of language, without which it would not have been possible.

Martin Buber, the Jewish philosopher, gives an example of a word in a primitive language which means "They stare at one another, each waiting for the other to volunteer to do what both wish, but are not able to do." All this is one word; it is a word which labels a primary experience before it has been analysed and broken up into its component parts. Highly developed languages are those which allow such experiences to be analysed with a great precision, even though they may need twenty-three words where one sufficed before. The more developed the language, the greater can be the degree of articulateness. But, as the primitive languages remind us, primary experiences of involvement in a situation can be known and recognised long before there is the means to make them articulate.

The point is an important one for religion because theologians are continually saying that the truth about God cannot be fully expressed; all our attempts to describe Him are inadequate. They appeal to an inarticulate knowledge, which theology tries to make as articulate as possible.

However, the main object of this discussion has been to stress that articulate knowledge is not the only kind of knowledge, but that our knowledge of any situation is articulate in varying degrees. Some elements of experience, those mostly tackled by science, can be related to one another in a highly articulate way; others less so. But even in the highly articulate sciences we cannot escape from our dependence on our inarticulate knowledge of the ordinary world. Insofar as science is an art, as was argued in the last chapter, the inarticulate element is extremely important. This applies not only to the individual scientist as he learns his job within the scientific community;

it applies to the whole scientific enterprise at the most basic level of all, that of searching for a rational explanation of experience. We are forced to use the notion of "rationality" without being able to specify precisely what it means or what are the rules for detecting it. No matter how articulate we make our laws of logic, they can only be used by those who already have an inkling of what it means to make sense of a thing.

To admit that there can be inarticulate knowledge clears away one of the basic theoretical objections to religion which is strongly felt nowadays. It allows us to believe that our gropings after the meaning of things and our sense of the mystery of existence are not simply mistakes and misunderstandings, to be removed by being a bit more scientific or applying the laws of logic more ruthlessly. It becomes possible to see how there can be a confused and partial knowledge of reality, which is genuine even though it cannot be brought within the bounds of science.

Not all such claims to knowledge need be taken with equal seriousness. The fact that knowledge is inarticulate does not put it beyond criticism. The history of any religion is in part the history of successive criticisms and refinements of its fundamental insights.

In primitive cultures, when men were intensely conscious of themselves as bound up with the rhythms of nature, nature supplied the answer to religious questionings. The rustle of the trees, the murmurings of water, the shapes of stones, all these were religiously significant. The cycle of the seasons, seed-time and harvest, birth and death and rebirth, these were the great themes of religion. Astrology flourished because the stars, being there, must have a meaning for men's lives; our modern word "influence" originally referred to the spiritual powers which were supposed to "flow in" from the heavens. The invisible threads which bound men to the stars were typical of men's complete involvement in their natural environment. And the essence of paganism was to accept this, and clothe it in religious terms.

Before science could flourish, this view of the world had to die. Even in its most highly developed form, in Aristotelian philosophy, it constituted a barrier to scientific progress. In a scientific culture, as opposed to a primitive one, men are still thought of as part of nature; but the emphasis is completely different.

Nature is to be known and understood, not by personal involvement and sympathy, but by impersonal investigation. The world is to be studied as a collection of objects, unrelated to man except insofar as he is one of them. In the earlier chapters of this book we have traced the growth and seen some of the limitations of this point of view. We have seen too its religious implications. Religious questionings remain, but science seems to leave no room for satisfactory answers. In a world made up of objects, God has to be thought of either as an object or as a concept. If the former, there seems to be less and less space for him in our scheme of things as scientific knowledge advances; if the latter, religion is a private fantasy. The essence of scientific atheism was to accept this view of man's relationship to nature necessitated by classical physics, to clothe it in religious terms, and to claim that God was no more—discarded as an unnecessary hypothesis.

In our own day, the era of post-classical physics, of relativity, of the recognition of the limits of science, dogmatic scientific atheism is dying and is being replaced by agnosticism. If science cannot disclose the ultimate truth, then neither can our religious questionings. The essence of agnosticism is to be aware of the limitation of human knowledge, to clothe it in religious terms, and to declare that no answers to religious questions are possible.

There remains, however, a fourth way of thinking about men's knowledge of the world, a way which leaves genuine scope for inarticulate knowledge, refined and criticised by science, and which is far more congenial than any of the other ways to the sort of religious answers given in the Bible. According to this fourth way, we know different facets of our experience in different ways and with different degrees of precision. There is a hierarchy of knowledge. At one end of the scale there is precise scientific knowledge of those features of experience which can be treated as objects existing independently of us; at the other end, there is the knowledge we have of other persons by our involvement with them, the kind of knowledge we can only have when we *stop* treating them as objects. At one end of the scale we have extreme articulateness; at the other end, extreme inarticulateness. And just as there is an inverse relationship between articulateness and involvement, so there is also a relationship between involvement and interest. When we stop thinking about knowledge in the abstract, we have to admit that what interests us most is what involves us most as persons. Quite apart from every other consideration, a world of which we only had precise scientific knowledge would be appallingly dull.

Paganism went wrong because it tried to come to terms with the world of objects through personal involvement; and it found gods in every bush. Scientific atheism went wrong, because it tried to reduce the whole of experience to our experience of objects. Agnosticism, I believe, goes wrong because it recognises the limits of knowledge, but is too certain about precisely where those limits lie. Religiousness is always liable to go wrong either by claiming knowledge of a quasi-scientific kind, or by imagining that wherever there is a mystery, there is God.

Religious knowledge belongs to the inarticulate end of the scale, and the kind of mystery which should concern it is therefore the mystery of our involvement with persons. And this is precisely what we find in the Bible. The struggle in the Old Testament between Baal and the God of Israel was on just this issue.

Baal was a nature god, worshipped in a variety of local shrines. The baal of a particular place was the Lord of that bit of land, who had to be propitiated if the crops were to flourish. Baalism was a typical form of paganism.

The God of Israel, on the other hand, was the God who had revealed Himself to a particular people through historical events, and who made moral demands upon them. He was not an object. He could not be known apart from His actions in relation to men. His only authorised name pointed men straight to the mystery of personality—I AM WHAT I AM.

In fighting against Baal the prophets were, in effect, persuading the Israelites to find God, not in the mysteries of nature, but in human history. They showed up, in the light of events, the impotence and moral degeneracy of baalism. By distinguishing between God and nature, they implicitly opened the way for men to have a responsible and moral attitude towards nature. In Old Testament times this led to a lack of interest in nature as such. The Jews were always more concerned, perhaps even excessively concerned, about God in contrast with the natural world. But I do not think it is too far-fetched to say that in the fulness of time it was the prophets' distinction between God and nature which made possible the rise of science.

In the next chapter I shall say more positively what is meant by religious knowledge. All I have tried to do here is to outline a view of knowledge which is at least compatible with the kind of religious faith to be found in the Bible.

Chapter 18

RELIGIOUS DOGMA

"Any stigma," wrote Dorothy Sayers, "will do to beat a dogma." She went on to argue in a famous essay that "the dogma is the drama", that Christianity is exciting and important, not in spite of its dogmatism, but because of it.

Hitherto in this book I have used the word "religion" in a rather general sense, and in the last few chapters I have been trying to suggest where such general religious questionings and insights fit into the whole structure of knowledge. It might seem from the discussion so far that religious insights can be valuable, provided they are not dogmatic; that what is opposed to the spirit of science is not religion as such, but religious dogmatism; and that anything but the vaguest form of Christianity runs into insoluble difficulties because dogma is inseparable from it.

The modern popularity of mysticism is a sign of the search for religion without dogma; and so, at a less exalted level, is the even more popular religion of decent living and non-attending church membership.

Why could Dorothy Sayers be so excited by Christian dogma, while very large numbers of equally intelligent people see it as the symbol of all that they distrust in religion? Partly because the word "dogmatic" can have quite different overtones for different people. In one sense, to call someone or something "dogmatic" is to imply an intellectual arrogance and insensitivity, a blindness to criticism, an unwillingness to give reasons for what is asserted, and an intolerance of other opinions. But when Dorothy Sayers wrote "the dogma is the drama" she was not implying this attitude of mind at all. She was excited by Christianity because she believed that it was not a matter of human opinion, but was given by God; it was dogmatic because it rested on quite concrete assertions about what God had done; it could be proclaimed without arrogance for the very reason that it was dogmatic, because it had been received, not manufactured by human wisdom.

When using the word "dogma", therefore, it is very important to strip it of its associations and try to see what is actually meant by it. It might prove to be true that Christianity's claim to be God-given always leads to dogmatism in the worst sense; but this must not be assumed from the start, and I do not believe myself that the one inevitably follows from the other, though unfortunately history provides many examples of it happening.

Christian dogma can best be understood when it is seen as the surprising, almost incredible, answer given by God to human religious questionings. It can only make sense to those who are asking the questions which it claims to answer. As soon as it is taken out of the context of these questions, and tabulated and condensed into a set of quasi-scientific assertions about the world, the way is open for dogmatism of the kind most people deplore. But within the context of the questions, its "givenness", and hence its dogmatism, is seen to be precisely what is needed.

In earlier chapters I have described Christian truth as a matter of personal insight, as being the kind of knowledge which changes us and makes demands upon us, as known within the community of faith, and as based on historical facts. I now want to try to weave all these elements together in the light of what I have just said about dogma. The clue to it all is in our understanding of personal relationships.

John Jones, let us say, is getting to know Mary Brown. If he was feeling pompous he might talk about "deepening his relationship" with her; but in fact he just likes going around with her. He likes the swish of her summer frock, the lights in her hair and the glint in her eye. He likes the feeling of no longer having to sit in a café alone, he likes the envious looks of his friends, he enjoys the pride of possession. In short, what attracts him at first are the changes in his own sensations. And as the days pass and his heart beats faster, he imagines that what he is going to receive are more and more pleasant sensations for his own satisfaction.

But Mary is not a passive little mouse. She has not the slightest intention of letting John treat her as a plaything. She has a mind and will of her own, and she uses them. John is given one or two painful reminders that if she is going around with him, it must be because he cares about her, and not because he enjoys his own sensations. In other words, Mary forces John to recognise her as a person, and not a thing. And John, because at heart he is not as selfish as he might seem, allows her to do it.

The friendship ripens. Their hearts beat faster still. They begin the mysterious and exciting process of discovering one another more deeply. They inwardly delight in their "specialness". Even the moments when they seem to be up against one another are appreciated as moments of revelation. John had always liked girls with fair hair and sparkling eyes; but Mary is—different. It is not her hair or her eyes or her dress or his own feelings of pleasure which attract him most now; it is Mary herself. He realises he is in love. Mary, of course, had known it weeks ago.

What does John mean when he says "I am in love"? First he realises that he has been gripped by an experience which has come to him through another person, not been manufactured by him. He has not worked himself up into a state of love with Mary; it happened, and he allowed it to happen. Years later when he and Mary are an old married couple we may find them talking about the way they seemed to be given to each other. Deep personal relationships are generally of this kind. Other people meet us and change us, often when we are least expecting it.

Secondly, by saying "I am in love", John links the tumultuous, chaotic, and sometimes frightening, feelings in his own heart with an experience which has been recognised and described throughout the history of mankind. Most of civilised society supports him in valuing these feelings, and encourages him to make them the basis for the commitment of his life to the one he loves. John lives within a community of faith (in this instance—faith in family life) which helps him to give shape to his personal insights and to translate them into action. Where the community prohibits or discourages him from doing what he likes with Mary, and then casting her off, the prohibitions, so the community claims, are to protect them both and to help their love to grow to maturity.

In this relationship are most of the elements which we have seen are to be woven together in our description of the Christian faith. It is personal, yet only known in its fulness within a community which seems to fence it round with interpretation and prohibitions. Faith is a response to what is given; it is not something manufactured by us, but called out from us by something else. To make the response is to be changed; it is to set out on a new way of life, charted many times before, yet genuinely new because each person's experience is unique. For a couple in love it is their "specialness" which makes this the most exciting thing which has ever happened to them, even though they recognise that falling in love is as old as creation. The Christian making his response of faith finds the same "specialness", the same newness, which is not in the least diminished by the fact that theologians have tried to express the whole thing tidily in their dogmas. Dogmas are not the objects of faith; they are the expressions of it; they are the charts left by those who have travelled the way before us and who would tell us about its possibilities and warn us of its dangers.

The parallel between believing in Christianity and falling in love is not exact, and if carried to its logical conclusion, might be very misleading. But, at least, having religious faith is more like entering into a personal relationship than, say, doing a scientific experiment. And the analogy helps us to see religious dogmas in their right context.

The starting point of Christianity is Jesus Christ, and the heart of it is personal relationship with God through Him. The New Testament shows us a life which astonished and gripped a body of disciples. Those who responded to Him in His lifetime found themselves led on, by a series of strange events surrounding His death, to see in Him the fulfilment of the religious hopes and longings of their people. He was not at all what they had been expecting; He shattered most of their previous ideas about what they wanted; yet they found in Him an answer to their needs, deeper and more exciting than any they could have imagined for themselves. This was not just a personal matter, though without their own personal response they would have experienced none of it; but they would have understood nothing, they would have interpreted it in no depth without the long religious history of their people, without their belief that God acted in history, without some of those very ideas about the Kingdom of God and His Messiah which the coming of Jesus revolutionised. In other words, the way they interpreted what gripped them depended on what they already believed, which in turn depended on the events which had gripped their forefathers in Old Testament history.

Jesus came to men who belonged to a community of faith,

and His coming was decisive for them because it fulfilled their faith. This is why they spoke of Him as the revelation of God, as God in action completing the work begun with Abraham and Moses. To read the New Testament is to feel some of the sense of excitement of those who wrote it, as piece after piece of their Old Testament faith fell into place.

But this was firsthand experience on the part of those who had known Jesus, and who knew what it was they were using the Old Testament to interpret. Others could only share it as they were told the facts at secondhand, and it is in this handing down of tradition that Christian dogma had its origins. Christianity is dogmatic because the essential facts on which it is based are facts of history known only through the testimony of those who witnessed them.

At a later stage, when Christianity began to move out of its original Jewish home, there was a further great period of discovery as Greek philosophy was pressed into the service of Christian thought, and, in the eyes of Christian apologists, was illuminated and fulfilled just as the Old Testament had been. But obviously the further Christianity moved from its Old Testament background, the greater was the danger that the original experiences and insights would be obscured or distorted. It was to protect them that dogma began to acquire its second function, that of warning would-be Christians against ideas or interpretations which in the end would dissipate the central Christian beliefs. For example, what seem to be highly confident statements about the nature of Christ in early Christian confessions of faith, are often in fact primarily negative statements. They are warnings that it is impossible to do justice to the mystery of Jesus Christ either by thinking about Him solely in human terms, or by thinking about Him solely in divine terms; they do not solve the mystery; they force it on our attention *as a mystery*; and in that sense they are as much confessions of ignorance as they are claims to knowledge. Hilary of Poitiers, writing in the fourth century about the doctrine of the Trinity, said, "The errors of heretics and blasphemers force us to deal with unlawful matters, to scale perilous heights, to speak unutterable words, to trespass on forbidden ground. Faith ought in silence to fulfil the commandments, worshipping the Father, reverencing with Him the Son, abounding in the Holy Spirit, but we must strain the poor resources of our language to express thoughts too great for words. The error of others compels us to err in daring to embody in human terms truths which ought to be hidden in the silent veneration of the heart."

Dogma, so understood, far from being an arrogant and uncritical assertion of knowledge, can be a protection against superficial explanations, a stimulus to look deeper. It is just this kind of protection against superficiality that, in the realm of personal relationships, society's rules about, say, sexual behaviour are intended to afford. Such rules can sometimes have an effect precisely opposite to what is intended. A sexuality dominated by conformity to rules can be as superficial as a religion preoccupied with dogmatic formulae. But, when seen in their proper context, both rules and formulae can be a stimulus to greater achievement and insight than would have been possible by any amount of undisciplined experiment and speculation.

Within personal relationships such rules and formulae have an essential place, and there is nothing quite parallel to them within the context of science. But this is only to emphasise what has been said repeatedly, that science and religion belong to different ends of the spectrum of knowledge; and therefore it is the greatest possible mistake to think of religious dogmas as if they were pieces of scientific knowledge obtained by some mysterious non-scientific means. Christian dogmas are the signposts which point us to Jesus as the place where God is to be found by those who seek Him.

Once that is grasped, the way is open to working out a new religious attitude towards the world of nature, the world investigated by science, which avoids the errors of confusing religion with science or imagining that science can give us the answers to religious questions. The story of science and religion is the story of those confusions, a story which has seemed to end in a world without God, or a world in which no final answer to our religious questions is possible.

Those who take Jesus Christ, rather than the world of nature, as the starting point of their search for God may find the world no less empty than their atheist or agnostic colleagues. However, for them this is not an invitation to despair but a programme for action. The God who is found supremely in one human life must be sought in faint reflection in every human life. The God who made one human life supremely meaningful can make every human life meaningful. The God who used the ordinary stuff of human life as the means by which He revealed Himself can make the ordinary world serve His purposes. But He does all this by inviting disciples, by winning men's co-opera-tion, rather than by forcing a pattern upon events. Perhaps Nietzsche was right when he said that what meaning there is in the world, we create for ourselves; but I believe he was wrong when he described such creation as arbitrary. Those who take their starting point in Christ find themselves commissioned to make sense of their experience, as He made sense of it, by using it for God.

This is one of the ways of understanding the Christian sacra-ments. The characteristic method of Christian worship is to take bits of the ordinary stuff of life, bread and wine and water, and raise them to a new level of significance. The action is not arbitrary; the sacraments are what they are because they stem from Christ; they are "given". But once given, the sacramental principle can be extended to the whole of nature. Natural things can be consciously clothed with a new meaning by relat-ing them to Christ. The world, which would be meaningless by itself, becomes a purposeful place as men make it so; and they are enabled to do this because they themselves find a purpose for their lives in the man whose life was wholly one with God.

A Christian who thinks like this can then see his vocation as an active process of "making sense" of the world. This is different from the passive scientific attempt to make sense of things, i.e. to understand them. The Christian attitude is to ask what we *ought* to make of them, what their possibilities are in a world responsible to God, how far they can be made the grounds of worship and thanksgiving. Scientific understanding has an important part to play in this process, because religion is always in danger of degenerating into fancifulness, and grasp-ing its satisfactions too cheaply. But scientific understanding by itself is only half the story. Knowledge must not be thought of as something detached from persons who know and act. Science searches for impersonal knowledge; Christianity insists that knowledge carries responsibilities, and that we only know the world truly as we use it rightly for God. Science empties the world of meaning; Christianity clothes it with meaning by find-ing its focus in Jesus Christ. Science gives us power; Christian-ity shows us the power of God in action in a rejected man on a cross; it turns upside down our ideas about the use of power.

These contrasts do not exclude one another. There is no need for science and Christianity to be in fundamental conflict. But in an age when conflicts lie not very far in the past, in an age of philosophical scepticism when all talk about knowledge and all attempts to be constructive are extremely tentative, there are bound to be tensions. It has been the argument of this book, however, that such tensions do not necessarily imply that one side is right and the other wrong. On the contrary, it is possible to be both an honest Christian and an honest scientist, and to find the two allegiances both illuminating and correcting one another.

BIBLIOGRAPHY

Allport, G. W., *The Individual and his Religion*, Macmillan, 1960.
A classic on the psychology of religion.

Barbour, Ian G., *Issues in Science and Religion*, S.C.M Press, 1966.
By far the best general textbook on the subject.

Barbour, Ian G. (ed.), *Science and Religion*, S.C.M. Press, 1968.
A wide and representative selection of essays by different authors.

Birch, L. C., *Nature and God*, S.C.M. Press, 1965.
Particularly interesting on Darwinism and creation.

Butterfield, H., *The Origins of Modern Science, 1300–1800*, Bell, 1949.

Clark, R. E. D., *Christian Belief and Science*, English Universities Press, 1960.
A popular account of how scientific discoveries are actually made, told in such a way as to emphasise the element of faith in all discovery.

Coulson, C. A., *Science and Christian Belief*, Oxford University Press, 1955.
A popular account of science as a form of religious activity. Suggestive but not entirely satisfactory.

De Lubac, H., *The Drama of Atheist Humanism*, Sheed and Ward, 1949.
A simple introduction to Feuerbach, Nietzsche, etc.

Dillenberger, J., *Protestant Thought and Natural Science*, Doubleday, 1960.
An excellent historical analysis of the ways in which Protestant views of the Bible were affected by the growth of science.

Gilkey, L., *Religion and the Scientific Future*, S.C.M. Press, 1970.
An exploration of the role of myth in science and theology.

Gillispie, C. C., *The Edge of Objectivity. An Essay in the History of Scientific Ideas*, Oxford University Press, 1960.
A major work on the effects of science on men's general conception of knowledge.

Heim, K., *Christian Faith and Natural Science*, S.C.M. Press, 1953.
An elaborate working-out of the analogy of different dimensions of existence. (See chapter 15 of this book.) Not all will approve its strong existentialist slant.

Hesse, M. B., *Science and the Human Imagination*, S.C.M. Press, 1954.
A concise discussion of the nature of scientific theories by a Christian philosopher of science.

BIBLIOGRAPHY 153

Kuhn, T.S., *The Structure of Scientific Revolutions*, Chicago, 1962.
   Already a classic on the scientific method.
Lack, D., *Evolutionary Theory and Christian Belief. The Unresolved Conflict*, Methuen, 1957.
   Short and very clear.
Polanyi, M., *Personal Knowledge. Towards a Post-critical Philosophy*, Routledge and Kegan Paul, 1958.
   A major philosophical work which attempts to rethink the philosophy of science. (See chapter 17 of this book.)
Pollard, W. G., *Physicist and Christian*, S.P.C.K., 1962.
   (See chapter 16 of this book.)
Schilling, H. K., *Science and Religion. An Interpretation of Two Communities*, Allen and Unwin 1963.
   A useful exploration of the general relationship between science and religion. Not much discussion of particular problems.
Teilhard de Chardin, P., *The Phenomenon of Man*, Collins, 1959.
   A difficult book, but the most comprehensive presentation of his thoughts about evolution. Should be read as a suggestive kind of scientific poetry.
Toulmin, S., *The Philosophy of Science*, Hutchinson, 1953.
   A simple exposition, with a positivist slant.
von Weizsäcker, C. F., *The World View of Physics*, Routledge and Kegan Paul, 1952.
   A discussion of the religious implications of modern physics. Strongly Kantian in outlook.
Whitehead, A. N., *Science and the Modern World*, Cambridge University Press, 1926.
   An old classic, worth reading for its historical parts.

Approaches to Religious Education

Margaret Evening

For the student about to take up a first teaching post, for the teacher with some years of experience but a little exhausted of ideas, for the youth leader and junior church teacher who need help with programme planning.

APPROACHES TO RELIGIOUS EDUCATION is packed with ideas and suggestions for lively lessons. It contains general discussions on the value of the thematic approach and team teaching, dance drama, model making, school assemblies and social service projects. It gives accounts of particular experiments in these fields and further practical information in the form of summaries of courses, detailed suggestions for life themes, scripts, hints on difficulties likely to be encountered and lists of useful books and films.

'*Margaret Evening has magnificent ideas and originality and a most refreshing knowledge of conditions in schools, and the practical details of daily encounters, staffroom tensions and relationships between girls and staff. There is much material in her book which will be of practical use to teachers in classrooms.*'

JANET R. GLOVER, Headmistress, Sutton High School for Girls.

MARGARET EVENING is a lecturer in Divinity at Gipsy Hill College of Education, Kingston.

£1.50 paperback, **£2.50** hardback.

Through the year with William Barclay

Edited by
Denis Duncan

Devotional readings for every day

WILLIAM BARCLAY was born in Wick in Caithness, Scotland, over 60 years ago. His father was a banker, and his godfather was that famous Scottish laird, Cameron of Lochiel. He was an only child. When he was five, his parents moved to Motherwell, in the heart of the Lanarkshire industrial belt.

He graduated with first-class honours in classics at Glasgow University, gained his B.D. at the same University and continued post-graduate study in Germany.

He was ordained in 1933, his first and only charge being on the fringe of Glasgow, in Renfrew on Clydeside. In 1946 he became a lecturer at Trinity College, and was called to the Chair of Biblical Criticism in 1963.

£2.00 net in U.K.